SIMPLE
Custom
WILD

STANISLAV SYNKO

Publisher, Copyright, and Additional Information

Simple Custom Wild by Stanislav Synko

ISBNs:
979-8-9893579-1-8 (Paperback)
979-8-9893579-0-1 (Hardcover)
979-8-9893579-2-5 (eBook)

Editing by Andy Earle & Nicole Taché
Cover design and interior design by Rafael Andres

Contents

Chapter 1:
I Got Swag, Baby

Imagine playing a game like Super Mario™ with no extra lives—and your entire net worth on the line. This is what it's like to run a start-up. Founders face new challenges constantly, and they can't make a wrong move. In the early days of a company's life, even basic mistakes can be fatal.

There are a million ways to make bad decisions in the process of starting a new company. You can hire the wrong key person, overpay for services, build a solution that doesn't scale well, waste time with the wrong contractor, ignore security and have a leak of personal user data. The list goes on. Because things evolve so quickly in a start-up, there are a massive number of decisions to make. There are forks in the road *everywhere*.

Founders are especially likely to make errors in judgment in areas where they lack expertise, like technology. Non-technical entrepreneurs can make disastrous mistakes when they lack a high-level understanding of the technology on which their start-up relies.

Except, unfortunately, that's *all* of us.

It's nearly impossible to start a company today without integrating *a lot* of technology. Every entrepreneur is, at least partially, in "tech." Every company uses technology for maintaining websites, conducting meetings, doing outreach, storing documents, and much more. Start-ups need tech to build products and scale revenue, but there's no way the founder can become an expert in all these various technologies.

This means entrepreneurs are often forced to manage and oversee the implementation and use of technologies they don't fully understand. They become prone to making simple mistakes. Things can quickly go astray when someone who lacks the necessary expertise is in charge of technology, and it happens all the time in the start-up world.

Thankfully, plenty of evidence shows it's possible to lead a company without having deep technical expertise in every aspect of the business. Many highly successful app founders do not write a single line of code. The CEO of Intel has never built a microchip with his bare hands. The president of a hospital likely couldn't diagram the inner workings of an MRI machine. **The secrets to running a company as a non-technical founder are out there…because plenty of people are doing it.**

Unfortunately, Jeremy Parker and Josh Orbach hadn't discovered any of those secrets when they founded their promotional products company SWAG.COM back in 2016. They were about to discover a hard truth about how costly it can be to not understand your tech.

SWAG.COM Founders Start Strong, But Experience Big Setbacks

Things started out great for Jeremy and Josh. Despite having over 30,000 competitors, the two young men hustled their way through the corporate office buildings of New York City and made $60,000 in sales with nothing but some business cards and a lot of chutzpah. They officially had some revenue. The next step was to build a website. That's where they hit their first major setback.

Jeremy had his heart set on the domain name SWAG.COM, but it wasn't available. Someone else already owned SWAG. COM and they refused to sell it for less than $1.2 million. Of course, the aspiring founders didn't have anything close to that. So, it seemed impossible for them to ever get the domain name SWAG.COM. This is where most normal people would give up. Not these guys.

The entrepreneurs wouldn't settle for anything other than SWAG.COM as their name.

"I had this vision of people seeing our ad in January, and not thinking about it for months," Jeremy said. "And then they are doing a big corporate event in August, and someone suggests getting swag, so they immediately think, 'Hey, I know where to get that.' And we had to be SWAG.COM so people could remember us all that time later."

The domain name was very important.

"It wasn't going to work without that," Jeremy said, shaking his head. "We had to be SWAG.COM. There was no way

3

around it."

With the seller asking for $1.2 million, and Jeremy and Josh sitting on just over $60,000 in assets, the two young founders wouldn't be able to buy the domain, even if they could negotiate the price down by half. However, a new investor was able to buy the domain from the original owner for $200,000—a bargain. But, SWAG.COM wouldn't quite be Jeremy and Josh's just yet.

The investor owned the domain name, and that's when Jeremy came up with a new way to set up the deal.

"I offered to pay back the $200,000 within two years," Jeremy remembers, "and also to give the guy a bit of equity in the company. Worst case scenario, if it didn't go anywhere, and we couldn't pay back the $200k, he'd get the domain back after two years and could do whatever he wanted with it."

The founders now had two years to get the company operational and earn at least $200,000.

Jeremy and Josh opened a WeWork office space on 42nd Street in New York City and hired a development firm to help them build a website. To keep things simple, they opted to build the initial site using a popular drag-and-drop shopping platform. This way, most of the online store could be made using pre-built options. They only had to build a plug-in that would add a few more advanced, custom features to the site.

They wanted the site to allow users to upload their logo or artwork and position it on a T-shirt, mug, calendar, or other item, then add text, preview a mock-up of the item, and place an order. It was a bit complicated because the site would have to consider factors like inventory, colors, materials, shipping costs, and more to calculate dynamic pricing for the customer in real time. The development team was confident they could handle it all and they started work.

Three months later, the website was 95 percent complete and Jeremy and Josh had spent about $25,000 on the project. They were expecting to receive the final version any day from the developers. That's when they learned some bad news.

"The developer called to explain that he couldn't finish the site," Jeremy says. "I was in shock. Apparently, the platform didn't support the dynamic pricing we needed. And he said his team had only just realized right at the end of the project that it's actually impossible."

So, Jeremy and Josh found themselves back at square one. They needed a website. Except, they had wasted three precious months and half of their money on code that was never going to work, and they weren't any closer to being able to pay back that $200,000.

Jeremy thought about how this catastrophe could have been avoided. *How come the dev team couldn't see this problem farther in advance? Was it a scam? Should I have hired a Chief Technical Officer?* Questions rattled in his head, and he knew he should've asked them back in January.

Just a small way into his entrepreneurial journey, Jeremy was already caught in one of the classic Founder's Dilemmas— he was hiring others to build something he didn't understand. And that's an easy way to make basic, avoidable mistakes.

You may be an expert in pottery. But, what about packaging? Or marketing? Or accounting? Maybe you're a gifted chemical engineer. But, how well do you understand safety regulations? And shipping logistics? No matter what kind of business you're in, and what amazing skills you have, at some point you'll have to hire someone to do something you don't understand. This is a key Founder's Dilemma.

In the case of Jeremy and Josh, they needed to build a website, but didn't understand much about software. This led them to make mistakes early on. Eventually, they realized they had to abandon the plug-in they'd expected to work and start over again with something brand new.

Jeremy and Josh aren't unique. The hurdles they faced in building a tech product, when neither of them knew how to write code, are the same issues that plague millions of entrepreneurs around the world. Their journey is emblematic of a greater struggle in the business world at large. Executives, who may not be technical, need to manage teams of people who are using complex stacks of tech products, manufacturing tools, and chemical processes. A Human Resources specialist may not understand how lasers work, but they need to hire an expert for a new project.

Thankfully, with so many people around the world struggling with these same limitations, some solutions have emerged. For example, in the start-up world, founders are notorious for mentoring each other and sharing ideas that work. In the collaborative culture of Silicon Valley, we love to fix difficult problems (and brag about how brilliant our solutions are). That helps maintain, and accelerate, the pace of innovation.

This book will help you overcome the Founder's Dilemmas

in the start-up world. You'll learn how to interpret the rapidly evolving technology landscape so you can avoid the kind of mistakes Jeremy and Josh made. You'll see that, for people building a tech product, a common pitfall is mis-categorizing their objective. They don't understand what *type of product* they are even trying to build. In this book, you'll learn a simple framework for getting this right from the very beginning.

About Me

You might be wondering how I developed this framework and, for that matter, who I am. I'm Stanislav Synko and I've dealt with the Founder's Dilemmas repeatedly during my career as a software engineer, architect, and tech CEO. I've founded two service companies to help start-up founders navigate their technology needs. In 2017, we made our first investment (you guessed it, in SWAG.COM).

Many entrepreneurs are highly skilled in areas like business, sales, and marketing, but not in technology. This is why it's so common for tech companies to have two founders. There's one more business-y person and one technical person. Gates had Allen. Jobs had Wozniak. Zuckerberg had Moskovitz. But, what about founders who are doing it alone? Plenty of people start successful companies by themselves. How can they get reliable technical advice?

This mission became the DNA of my venture studio, Aleph One. We work to help founders understand the different technological options for building their product. We guide them through big decisions of tech strategy, team design, and phasing. Essentially, we function like a CTO and a tech team for companies who don't have a technical co-founder. The cherry on top is our investment piece. I realized there was a need for a company in the service tech industry that has its incentives aligned with entrepreneurs, participating in funding rounds and not just providing high-quality tech service.

When I first met Jeremy and Josh, they were frantic to fix their broken website and I was desperate to find work for my small development company. We worked out a deal to completely rebuild the platform using a custom backend. Within a few months, SWAG.COM was online and orders were rolling in.

Over the following years, I worked closely with the SWAG.COM team to add new features to their site. To solidify the partnership, Aleph One even made an investment in the start-up when they decided to raise capital. As the company grew, they never needed to hire their own in-house development team—Aleph One handled that. Today, more than 35 Aleph One engineers support their tech needs, making SWAG.COM one of the industry leaders.

Things have come a long way for SWAG.COM. In 2022 the company earned over $40 million in sales. They were recently acquired by Custom Ink, a major player in the industry. They have long since outgrown their tiny WeWork office space on 42nd Street and now have distribution centers across the country. As for the $200,000 due to the original owner of the SWAG.COM domain? That's been paid in full.

Since the success of SWAG.COM, many founders have approached me about similar partnerships. They want Aleph One to invest in their start-up and to help develop their technology, too. To make things interesting, by investing in our clients, we put some skin in the game so they know we are always going to act in their best interests, rather than trying to find ways to upcharge them for more development work. We want them to be profitable, because when our clients get acquired, we share the upside with founders and are rewarded for the long journey we've taken together.

During my journey with Aleph One, I've constructed a solution to a key Founder's Dilemma—the dilemma of having expertise in areas like business, sales, and marketing, but not in technology. It's a practical solution, but it will require some work on your part. It requires analyzing your project in depth to understand your tech needs. Sometimes you might actually be able to build the product yourself if the right tools exist. Other times, you might need to hire a full-time technical genius to oversee development. Often, you can get away with an external tech team, if you can keep priorities aligned.

So, how do you know which type of product you're building? How can you assess your own tech needs? How can you determine when you need to outsource and when you really need to hire a new in-house employee, or learn for yourself? What's the first step to take when you find yourself stuck in this key Founder's Dilemma?

Let's dive in…

The Three Types of Tech Products

I've spent the better part of my career advising start-ups on their technology implementation. In this time, I've found it extremely useful to divide all tech products into three main categories, based on the nature of their technology needs: Simple, Custom, and Wild West.

I've noticed these are the three distinct tracks a product can take to maturity, depending on how the technology is used to solve its customers' problems. Heading down the wrong path is a costly mistake that many small start-ups never recover from. When founders don't understand which type of product they are building, they can easily pursue strategies that directly conflict with the product's true technology needs.

I have conversations with founders every day, often about securing funding and/or technical resources, and I constantly see the same three types of products in start-ups:

Simple

A Simple product is something an average person could potentially make on their own using existing and out-of-the-box tools.

Custom

For a Custom product, the company has built a custom software platform, which gives them an edge over their competitors in an established industry.

Wild West

There is an extreme level of innovation for these products, to the point where the company is creating a new business model or inventing a new type of technology—hence, I refer to this level of product as Wild.

Just this morning, I spoke with two different entrepreneurs who have two very different levels of technology requirements. The first company built a mental health wellness app for pediatricians and their patients. This is a Custom product because they are innovating within an existing industry, consumer healthcare services, and have built a custom software platform. The second company helps scientists extract meaning from bioinformatics datasets, like genomic data. Their product is deeply innovative and requires technical genius to pull off. They are absolutely a Wild product. This particular founder is non-technical, but he has partnered with someone who has expertise in AI, data science, and natural language models to help build the product. For Wild products, it's critical to partner with an expert in the technology.

While these three types of products may seem obvious, it's amazing how many founders have misconceptions about what type of product they are building, and what technology they need.

A perfect example of this involves me and my good friend Pavel. He was starting up a media company, based in New York City, with content distributed through their website. He hired my team to build a custom editorial platform. We spent 18 months working on a highly advanced editorial functionality for his articles. He had a creative vision to re-imagine the process of content creation. There were different types of editors, and different steps in the process, and a whole lot going on.

He wanted software that tied everything together.

First, we started with a basic WordPress site, but Pavel soon flew past the limits of complexity with that platform. So, we built a custom platform that allowed us to implement features like dynamic ad placement, advanced analytic tools, and a custom flow of editing articles sequentially, by many parties. Admittedly, the platform is very creative. It can produce fun content. Still, at the end of the day, it allows people to write and publish articles.

There are many other existing software platforms that support collaboration between groups of writers, an editorial process, and publication to a blog. The technology doesn't really make any extra money. It was not a software company. The fancy process isn't being licensed to other media companies. It's purely for internal use.

Things became more complicated than they had to be. It began as a Custom product, but we really could have kept it Simple. My biggest regret from that time was that I didn't have the experience to push back and disagree with Pavel. If I could do it again, we would approach it differently from the start. I would tell him that I don't think this fancy technology will help the business. I shouldn't have said yes to all of his requests so easily. As a media company, what we really needed was marketing and readership. We needed to get more eyes on his content and get people sharing it across other platforms. The system we spent 18 months working on was way more complicated than it had to be.

When entrepreneurs misjudge the level of technology they

will need to implement to bring their product to the market, the results can be swift and cold. **Founders who thoroughly understand their tech requirements can make the right moves at the start and blow past the competition.**

Let's take a closer look at each type of product.

Simple Products

The most technologically basic type of product is one that a typical person would be able to make for themselves without much trouble. There is no rocket science here. This is a situation where you can use pre-built solutions that don't require any coding knowledge. At this level, you don't have any custom features that need to be developed on top of the platform.

The biggest benefit of pursuing a Simple product is that it doesn't cost much to build, so an entrepreneur can theoretically make it without needing to raise capital. The costs to get a Simple product up and running could easily be put on a regular credit card. Mainly, it's just the founder's time that goes into making the initial version.

As technology evolves, more products are becoming Simple. It's actually quite "simple" to mistake a product as Simple because you're familiar with another product that does something similar to what you're planning. "Hey, if those guys are doing that, surely we can do this, right?" Often, it seems like it should be easy to build on top of existing products and make a few tweaks. But, software development doesn't always work like that.

The story of SWAG.COM is a perfect example of company

founders who thought they could build a Simple product, but actually needed to develop a custom platform and thus needed to build a Custom product. They wasted three months and $25,000 hoping to salvage their Simple solution, made on a popular e-commerce platform. Instead, they would have been much better off working on a custom platform right from the start. Their product required advanced business logic, ware-housing, dynamic pricing and an innovation in the supply chain to deliver branded products to their customers. This easily places their product in the Custom category.

Often, an idea seems like it will be simple to build at first, but then after getting started it becomes apparent that it's going to be a huge challenge. On the other hand, it can be wise to begin with a more simple version of the product, rather than jumping right into full-scale development of a Custom or Wild product. Sometimes this "simple version" could just be a landing page to gauge interest and collect email addresses. Anything that can be built by an average person without much trouble is potentially a Simple product.

Custom Products

When a company gets to the point where it is building its own custom software platform, it has officially crossed over to build-ing a Custom product. These organizations are writing code to develop their own solution to a problem, and their unique software becomes part of their competitive advantage. They are enhancing existing business models and supply chains. Similar things have been done before, but not exactly *this*.

Custom products are based on a proven business model.
When deciding whether a product falls into this category, one
of the most obvious questions to ask is whether the company
that is building it has any competitors. If there are competitors
who are successfully turning a profit, there is no reason a new
company shouldn't be able to capture some market share and
carve out a niche. In this case, the new software platform (i.e.,
the Custom product) should give the company an edge to
compete in the established industry. On the other hand, if the
product does something nobody else is doing, and doesn't fit
into an existing business model, it's likely Wild—we'll discuss
this product type later.

While building Custom products is not as easy as building
Simple products, the process is fairly straightforward. A new
platform, for example, is similar to other existing products,
so engineers can follow the conventions of other successful
platforms to design and develop your product. It's much easier
to visualize the roadmap to a complete product when developers are making something similar to other projects they've
done before.

One big factor that differentiates the three types of products is how much they cost to build. While a Simple product
is relatively cheap to assemble—between a few hundred and a
few thousand dollars—a Custom product requires a more significant budget. This means the founder will have to either raise
capital, make a sizable investment themselves, earn revenue
from another form of business, win the lottery, or somehow
find a way to cover the development costs. In general, it's going

to cost at least $100,000, and could scale quickly, to build this type of product. Companies building Custom products might raise about a quarter million to a million dollars during their first funding round. Companies building Simple products, however, will usually need less than $100,000 (sometimes even under $10,000) to get going, and the founders often cover this themselves, or borrow it from friends and family.

In total, across all rounds of funding before acquisition, SWAG.COM raised about $3.5 million. This might seem like a lot of money, but it's actually not that much in the realm of valuable platforms. The company ultimately sold for many times that amount. This is a pretty typical volume of capital to raise for a company that is building a Custom product.

As we mentioned, savvy entrepreneurs will often start with a Simple product to test an idea and see how people respond, before moving on to build what they know is a Custom product. If there is a favorable reaction to the Simple product, the founder can either directly use the profits to build a Custom product, or use the promising results to raise capital from investors, or both.

When Jeremy and Josh came to me in the midst of their problems starting up SWAG.COM, I immediately saw they were putting their product on the wrong level. They were building a Simple product, when they needed a Custom one. There was no way an off-the-shelf platform would stand up to all of the customizations they wanted.

For one thing, they had an insane number of products available for purchase. And, the user was supposed to be able to upload their logo and place it on the product. Their platform also prompted changes to the order flow depending on the specific type of product. For example, ordering custom T-shirts would prompt a different flow than ordering custom hoodies or mugs. The site also had to display live inventory data throughout a convoluted supply chain and production process. The technology was even supposed to automatically coordinate with manufacturers and shipping centers to manage inventory and order fulfillment all the way through to delivery.

As soon as I heard all of this, I knew they needed a fully custom platform. In fact, they even needed their own API. Any time a company has to build their own API it's definitely not a Simple product. It's either Custom or Wild.

Another example of a Custom product is Booking.com. It was certainly possible to book hotels before booking.com was created, but this innovative product shook up the entire travel and hospitality industry with its custom solution that catered not only to travelers but also owners of estates.

Is It Time to Hire a Full-time CTO?

Building a custom platform in any industry is a challenge, but that doesn't mean it requires a full-time CTO right away. In fact, one big mistake many founders make is hiring a CTO too early. This can actually be a huge problem because executives are expensive, and every dollar counts at a start-up. Additionally, a full-time CTO isn't necessary at this point. While there are certainly some important technical decisions to be made in these early stages, there is realistically only an hour or two of actual CTO work in a week, tops. Yes, you need some kind of partner who understands the tech and can advise you, but you don't need a full-time CTO yet.

Wild Products

Products that involve inventing new technology or developing an innovative business model are known as Wild products. This type of product requires significantly more expertise and capital to produce. Even though Wild products involve very complex technology, it's important to keep them as simple as possible.

One obvious sign that a product is Wild is that new technology has been invented. If any aspect of a product is something you would be able to patent, that's a Wild product. You've created something revolutionary. If your product involves AI, augmented reality, virtual reality, robotics, 3D printing, NFTs, or blockchain, it's almost certainly Wild. Another way to think about it is when a company considers a novel technology to be part of its competitive advantage, that's a Wild product.

The same is true from a business perspective, as well. Sometimes a product comes along that introduces an entirely new business model. Think Apple, Microsoft, Dell, Intel, DeepMind, Google. If you're developing a product that genuinely doesn't have any competitors because nobody else is doing what you're doing, that's a Wild product. Look around for examples of other companies that are successfully doing the same thing you're envisioning, or something very similar. If you can't find any, that might mean you're creating an entirely new business model. Welcome to the Wild.

While hiring a full-time CTO is a waste of resources at a company building a Simple product, it's a must at a start-up building a Wild product. **The biggest misconception at this level is that you can outsource your innovation to someone you don't know.** It's a big mistake to hire a development team without a full-time tech genius onboard to keep an eye on the big picture. The team will run around in circles and waste money. If you aren't a tech genius and you have a Wild kind of idea, start looking for a CTO or technical co-founder fast.

Of the three types of products, a Wild product is the most costly to build, by far. For one thing, you'll need to employ one CTO or tech co-founder who can scale the team. And tech geniuses are expensive. Also, companies pursuing Wild products tend to require cutting-edge technology, which can be priced at astronomical levels. To complicate things further, the timeline for building a Wild product is often vague, because nothing quite like this has ever been done before. And, time is money.

I met a guy the other day who is building a new type of blockchain. He is currently raising his first round of funding—$5 million. That's just one round. He'll need multiple rounds to do everything he's planning.

Plus, he won't make any money until the platform is fully functional. That's quite a lot of capital considering SWAG.COM only raised $2 million in total, across all rounds of funding. This is a big difference between Custom and Wild products.

The company Anthropic raised over $700 million to build an AI platform before even having a product out. They have over 10 publications in peer-reviewed AI journals, but they are not anywhere close to completing their product.

A while ago, some founders came to me for help in building a yacht marketplace app where users could rent out their boats. I thought it was a great idea. Then I heard that they wanted to use blockchain technology. The founder got excited as he explained how the company issued tokens to give clients discounts and incentivize customer loyalty and exclusive access. The basic idea of a yacht marketplace app was a pretty straightforward Custom product. But, adding in blockchain technology pushed things into the Wild category.

When they'd finished explaining the idea, I smiled and said, "This sounds great…for someone who doesn't understand technology. But, honestly, from an architecture perspective it makes no sense to incorporate blockchain so deep into this product."

The room got very quiet and they both turned to glare at me. I gulped. The silence was excruciating. Then, after an agonizing moment, they both broke into smiles.

"Hey, I like you!" They laughed. "You're no bullshit."

In this situation, I did what I wasn't able to do all those years ago with Pavel. I pushed back and advocated *against* the client's ideas.

The product ultimately ended up using light integration

of a blockchain. The platform is practically the same for all users, with a small marketing tool that engages blockchain users to get discounts if they've got tokens. That's it. This kept the product in the realm of Custom.

Even in the Wild category, it's still important to build a simple product. In fact, focusing on simplicity may be even more critical at this level because when a company pursues highly revolutionary ideas, it's easy for things to get too complicated. Remember what you value most. Don't get pulled away from your core mission. **Make sure you are solving one very specific problem for your customers.**

Don't Get Your Type Wrong

There are two ways a founder can be wrong about the technology required to build a product: overestimating or underestimating. Each of these scenarios can be disastrous. Some founders also overcomplicate their products, adding AI and blockchain in places that don't make sense or inventing new business models unnecessarily. Others oversimplify things, imagining it will be much easier to build features than it turns out to be. In all of these cases, the actions founders take are misaligned with the steps that will propel the company toward success.

Overestimating the Product

Imagine you assume a certain product is Custom (but, it's actually Simple because there is an existing platform that has almost all of the features you're looking for). You hire a development team to build a custom platform for you. And you spend months working with the UX designer on renderings, providing feedback to the software engineers, and testing the software for bugs. Finally, close to a year later, you're ready to launch.

While you were doing all of that, maybe a competitor quickly built a site using a basic no-code platform in two weeks and spent the rest of the year marketing, forming partnerships, and making sales. So, even though you are only just starting out after a year of working on your site, you're really a year *behind* other business owners who correctly assessed their technology needs as Simple right from the beginning. You spent a bunch of money, ramped up a high burn rate, missing a decent piece of equity because of an investment round and have overcomplicated your platform.

Another serious miscalculation can occur when a founder thinks their product is Wild, but it's really just Custom. There are many recent examples of start-ups trying to build their own data science models when a majority of generic machine learning models are solved and available to use via simple APIs. (We'll discuss AI innovation in more detail in Chapter 10.) These start-ups could spend over a million dollars on revolutionary technology. Or, they could use existing APIs that can do most of what they want. The quicker a founder realizes they are overestimating their product's technology needs, the better.

I talked to a founder last week who is raising a few million dollars to build a platform for purchasing reactive agents for biochemistry labs. She's planning to build a huge, custom e-commerce platform. If built from scratch, it's going to cost a fortune and take up a lot of time and energy. She doesn't really need to do all of that. Instead, she could research multi-vendor marketplace software online and likely get a platform running for under $10,000. She thinks she is planning a Custom product, but really it is Simple.

Underestimating the Product

The situation gets equally scary when the tables are turned. When entrepreneurs underestimate the complexity of their product, rather than overestimating it, things tend to go wrong in a different way. Think of how it might play out if you assumed your product was Simple when it was actually Custom. You might go ahead with building it yourself. You'd create a WordPress site and install lots of plug-ins to achieve the many features you envisioned. You'd likely end up piecing together a collection of different technologies to make the site work. As time goes on, you'd realize there are not enough plug-ins or customization features to make all pieces work together. It feels like wearing clothes that are held together with a single, fraying piece of thread.

Using too many different technologies together in one product is an invitation for things to break. Each additional plug-in or service that gets added to a site, for instance, makes it more fragile and difficult to scale overall. In mission critical environments, these products tend to fail. When this happens, the damage to your reputation or cashflow can be irreparable.

The Problem with Buying Existing Software

Consider this example. One client wanted to build a platform that could compete with MailChimp, a popular software that enables users to send email blasts to large lists of subscribers. He was setting out to create a Simple product when he was actually envisioning a Custom product.

He thought he would be able to buy some generic, bulk email software and hire a developer to make a few tweaks to it. Except, he had a very specific vision of exactly how he wanted every little detail of the platform to work. He also had a lot of ideas, like integrating a custom supply chain, holding giveaways, and allowing users to run different types of ad campaigns.

The big problem with purchasing existing software is that it is resistant to change. There are really two ways to change existing software: hire the same team that built it to change it, or hire someone else to do it for you. Both options are problematic.

Option 1: Hiring the original team.

If a company is selling software cheaply, they are probably selling it "as is," meaning they would have a high price tag on customization. Also, they are probably customizing

---

their software for many companies like yours. So, they might be quite jammed keeping up with many product versions and clients. I've never had a good experience with hiring the original teams behind cheap software.

Option 2: Hiring someone else.

This option is problematic for two reasons: code quality and code stability. You know how you lose a warranty on a car if you try taking it to an unauthorized dealer for a fix while it is still under warranty? Same goes with software—if you change it, you're putting its stability at risk. Making an engineer responsible for changing a decent chunk of existing software carries not only stability risk, but also inability to get updates after purchase, as well as infrastructure and security risks. Not to mention how changes would impact the scaling of such software.

In summary: Only buy software if you are ready to use it "as is," and only if it has been proven to be stable by other clients in live products for a long period of time.

Overcomplicating the Product

These days, people frequently tell me they want to build their own blockchain. I think some people imagine fad technologies work somewhat like hot sauce. Can't you just add a dash of blockchain to any app idea? Won't it make everything taste better? Can you sprinkle some machine learning on top and serve it on a bed of artificial neural networks?

This signals a misunderstanding of how big an undertaking it is to build a blockchain. Some imagine this might be something like a Custom project, or even Simple. Shouldn't there be off-the-shelf blockchain solutions by now? In reality, any product that includes blockchain integration is Wild. Integrating a blockchain is such a huge architecture, infrastructure, and software task, it has to be Wild. It involves cryptography, performance computing, distributed computing—not exactly stuff you can figure out by watching a few YouTube videos.

A similar phenomenon plays out with AI as well. Some people just throw AI into their pitch deck, thinking it could only make the idea sound better. What could be sexier than AI? Everything suddenly feels more cutting edge when it has AI integrated. If an idea is good on its own, it could only be better with AI, right? Founders jump from what would have been a very basic Custom product to a difficult, overcomplicated Wild product.

That being said, use of AI is picking up rapidly with emerging no-code tools that allow you to build comprehensive models to integrate into your product. This means a lower bar for entry, but also easier integrations down the line, which would keep Custom products from entering the Wild category.

I had two different people in my office last week with the same problem. Both said they wanted to build their own blockchain (yeah, you'd be surprised at how many of those we get). But, neither of them had technical expertise in blockchain networks. They both had the attitude that it should be easy to find someone to develop the software. Also, both entrepreneurs had already spent over $50,000 on software development.

These two founders didn't realize they were stepping into the world of Wild products. They didn't need to look for a development team, they needed to hire a full-time tech genius to advise them in exchange for a share in their company, or a combination of salary and vested equity if they are hiring someone they don't know. Using freelancers to build a truly revolutionary product doesn't generally work all that well. Freelancers do what they are told. For more abstract projects, you can't tell collaborators exactly what to do. They need to get creative.

Move On Up

A product doesn't have to stay at the same level forever. In fact, some products progress from Simple to Custom, and then gradually up to Wild. A Simple product is much easier to start, but a Wild product leads to a better valuation. So, there is a strong incentive to climb the ladder and push the value of the product higher.

Investors generally calculate the value of a company based on a certain multiplier of its revenue. A company with a Simple product would have a lower multiplier than one with a Custom or Wild product. This is because a Simple product is actually less competitive—widely available technology doesn't give you any real edge over the competition. Anyone could easily copy your product tomorrow if it was so simple to make. On the other hand, a company with a custom platform would command a significantly higher revenue multiplier because their software gives them a unique advantage. For Wild products, the size of the multipliers can be sensational.

One good example that shows how company valuations can vary is our client who does small business loans. Many small businesses make money, but don't have access to loans, so this company will lend them money through their app. They built an entire custom platform to manage their operations and perform faster due diligence. They now have automated tools for onboarding new clients, too. They are called Paintbrush (getpaintbrush.com). Reach out to them if you need $50,000 debt financing and tell them I sent you!

SMB (small business) lending is a tough space. Here, you don't usually get past conservative multiples of 1.5x-2x revenue. Innovators like Paintbrush, though, who have everything automated may get a true tech company multiple of 7x or more.

Another good example of varying company valuations is SWAG.COM. Conventional branded product companies are old school. They have been around for a long time. These types of businesses typically get low multipliers, in the range of .5-times to 1.5-times revenue. But, SWAG.COM sold for well over 2x. They are now working on developing a brand-new business model within their industry, so they may move into Wild soon.

Most unicorns valued at more than $1 billion are in the Wild category. However, it comes with a price. Most start-up failures occur in this category. It is extremely hard to pull Wild products off the ground. If you're going to be disrupting business models, it's good to start conservative. You can get established, learn the market, make connections, look for sources of cash flow, and gradually build up to Wild. This way, you have a solid foundation on which to build some crazy dreams.

So, what does it take to build Simple, Custom, or Wild products? The following chapters will explore key strategies and tools needed to build each of the product types, moving gradually from somewhat obvious topics like website builders to the wild world of AI innovation. My goal is to inspire you to become a little bit more technical and to be more confident about the areas of your product that you don't know, yet.

Are you ready to get to work?

Chapter 2:
Avoid Oversights with Simple Tech

Regardless of the type of industry, a basic understanding of simple technology can set a business on a solid foundation. Non-technical founders can accomplish much with simple technology—what I call "simple tech." With simple tech, founders can create a website and set up a company email address in a day. They can streamline internal communications using a cloud-based platform. They can submit the required paperwork to open a business bank account or sign client contracts without leaving their home office. These are essential pieces of simple tech every company needs.

Although this technology is simple, small oversights can cost founders hundreds of thousands of dollars down the road. There are surprising ways its utility can be overlooked. One stolen administrative password can lead to a broken ecommerce site. A single missing financial document could lead to a hefty IRS fine. In this chapter, we'll look at a few examples of such oversights and how you can avoid them.

Ecommerce sites, media production sites, service-based businesses, and brick-and-mortar stores can all be built on simple tech without the help of a Chief Technology Officer (CTO). Throughout this chapter, we'll explore simple tech tools I consider to be the gold standard (at the time of writing). Any non-technical founder can integrate these simple tech tools into their budding business.

To some readers, the value of simple tech might sound obvious, or even boring, but to other readers, simple tech might not sound so simple. A fair number of non-technical founders have no idea what an API is. (Answer: An "application programming interface," or API, is a way for different software to communicate.) So, while the technology we'll discuss in this chapter is relatively simple, it's still worth paying close attention to.

While the technology itself may be complicated, *using* it can be surprisingly straightforward. Software that optimizes standard business processes is objectively simple. Setup may take a day or two (and include watching a few video tutorials), but this is still faster and cheaper than custom technology. As soon as the technology is customized, a company enters the realm of custom tech, even if it is not vital to the company's operations, and the costs can quickly add up.

Every company will utilize simple tech to some degree, and even the most advanced companies may make costly mistakes by improperly setting up their simple tech. So, what are the basics of simple tech and what are the common mistakes and oversights to watch out for? I'll start to answer that question by sharing an ugly surprise a client of mine discovered years after their company's launch.

First, Research Your Domain Name

I once had a client in San Francisco who raised $2 million for a video marketing platform—they had a brilliant idea and a strong business model, but an oversight on simple tech set them back thousands of dollars. The client's company involved a lot of custom technology, but instead of fast-tracking innovation on their product, they spent time and money salvaging their brand.

For two years, my company built out the custom tech platform for this San Francisco client. We helped the company grow, but they plateaued much sooner than they projected. Their investors were expecting a 10x return on the initial $2 million raised, but the company was struggling to break even. What was the problem?

They had everything their business model suggested they would need—a fully functioning website, a dedicated sales team, active marketing campaigns—but they were failing to bring on new users organically from their website.

The company dug deep to figure out what was discouraging users to sign up on their site, and this eventually led them to an uncomfortable revelation. It happened when they researched backlinks to their website. There were millions! Where did all these backlinks come from? It turns out the previous website under their domain name was an adults-only site with fairly graphic content.

There was no way they could comb through all the sketchy, unwanted backlinks and eliminate them. Even if they could, the company had lost confidence in their own brand's image and was embarrassed. Finally, they accepted their fate. The company rebranded and remarketed to the tune of approximately $200,000—plus countless lost hours and stunted growth.

Most non-technical founders jump at the chance to buy the domain that is their business name. It follows that if a company is named "Johnson Brothers" and the domain "johnsonbrothers.com" is available, the company should buy it. However, no matter how benign or salacious a brand name may sound, companies will want to research the history of their desired domain name. For example, many companies with the letter "X" may find themselves in a similar position as my San Francisco client, purchasing domain names with questionable previous listings.

Researching a domain before purchase requires a bit of work, but not much. The reason for the research is that founders should know who last owned the domain and what was done with it. What other web pages are linked to the domain? The types of backlinks to a domain can dramatically influence the volume and frequency of traffic to a website.

Explicit content is not the only baggage to look out for when researching a domain name before buying it. Here is a practical checklist for domain name research:

- Check the domain's history using a tool like DomainTools, Whois, or Internet Archive. See if it was used for anything inappropriate or spammy in the past. This can prevent costly rebranding later.

- DomainTools provides a comprehensive history and overview of any domain's ownership and status. It can uncover hidden issues with a domain.

  - Internet Archive's Wayback Machine shows historical snapshots of websites and can reveal past uses of a domain.

  - Whois databases provide ownership and registration details of a domain, which can indicate if it was registered recently and potentially for the purpose of resale.

- Watch out for cybersquatting—which is the act of registering domain names in hopes of selling them later at a high price. Do some research to ensure the domain is not on any lists of known cybersquatted domains.

- Check for any pending litigation on the domain. There are tools to check Uniform Domain Name Resolution Process (UDRP) cases, which handle domain disputes. Ensure the domain is "clean" before purchasing. UDRPsearch is the tool for this.

- Do a Google search for the exact domain name and related keywords to see what comes up. This simple task can reveal a lot about the domain's history and suitability. Look for results that may indicate spam or other bad faith uses.

- Consider alternate top-level domains (TLDs) like .io or .co if the .com version has issues. Rebranding to a new TLD still requires effort and investment.

- Consulting a domain broker or consultant can also help evaluate domains, especially for expensive purchases. Their expertise aids in avoiding issues.

Whichever domain name a company chooses, I recommend everyone purchase and register the domain on one of the big domain registration platforms. The big names in domain registration (at the time of writing) are GoDaddy, Namecheap, and Google Domains. The main reason I recommend companies register with one of these top sites is that these domain registrars are accredited by ICANN.

ICANN accreditation ensures the domain registrar companies follow strict guidelines and standards for domain registration and management. Also, you can expect bonus features and ease of use from the top players. For example, Google Domains pairs seamlessly with email registration through Gmail. It only takes a few clicks to set up Gmail for a domain purchased through Google, whereas a smaller unknown registrar will require manual DNS ("Domain Name System") configuration.

You can save your company tons of time and money (and face) by researching a domain before purchasing it. But a squeaky-clean domain is not the only way you can avoid costly pitfalls with simple tech.

Website Builders Save Time and Money

Once you've purchased your well-researched domain name, the next step is to build your website. Contracting out the development of a custom platform to freelance developers automatically qualifies as custom technology and, in many cases, is unnecessarily complicated and expensive. Most basic websites can be built on templated host sites, allowing you to create the site you need without writing a single line of code. This is simple tech at its best, but there are still decisions to make that will influence your company's scalability down the road.

There are numerous website builders to explore. Review the options and make a decision *based on your business type*, not on the tool. Consider the following list of business types and leading options for website builders (prices noted reflect costs at the time of writing).

Ecommerce

Retailers who don't want the hassle of a brick-and-mortar shop can turn to ecomsmerce. Some retailers begin on sites like Etsy, Amazon, or eBay and, as they see success, transition to their own online store. Others, jump straight into an online shop. The right ecommerce website can help a retailer retain more of the profits, better track customers and sales trends, and increase brand awareness.

The leading options for ecommerce startups are Shopify, BigCommerce, Wix, and Squarespace. They all provide beautiful site templates, scalable platforms and integrations with payment gateways, shipping carriers, and other services an online store needs. Retailers who offer more customizable products may require the aid of a web developer, but using a specialized ecommerce platform saves time and money versus building a custom website from scratch.

Even multi-million-dollar companies like Kylie Cosmetics or Gymshark use Shopify, proving it can scale with a business. The costs range from free tiers to $2,000+ per month depending on features. Transaction fees may also apply. For most startup stores, the basic plans will be sufficient.

Media

For media startups like blogs, podcasts, or video channels, there are several great web-building tools. WordPress, Ghost, and Webflow are affordable and make it easy to create a content-focused website with support right out of the box. Many of the offered themes and layouts can be modified and redesigned without code.

Webflow and Ghost offer higher quality designs and are often quicker to set up. It might take more time to set up a WordPress website, however, WordPress offers more features and third-party integrations. Many successful media brands—from The Verge to Nerdist—still use WordPress, as custom development can expand its functionality.

If you're building a subscription-based media site, you'll need to use a membership plug-in like MemberPress (WordPress) or MemberSpace (Webflow), or a built-in member program with Ghost. These options integrate with payment gateways to charge subscribers monthly or annually and provide access control to premium content.

Brick-and-Mortar and Service-Based Businesses

For brick-and-mortar businesses like restaurants, shops, or service-based companies, the needs for online visibility are usually simple: an attractive website with contact and location information, and perhaps online booking. In this case, choosing a website builder based on design is usually most important.

Wix and Squarespace provide stunning templated designs tailored for these types of businesses. For the simplest websites, their basic plans will work. While custom development will not likely be needed, having an option to easily modify your site as your business grows is important. Both Wix and Squarespace make DIY changes simple and provide support if help is needed. Either builder is an excellent choice for a local business looking for an attractive, low-cost website.

In sum, choosing a website builder depends on your business model and needs. Ecommerce stores should opt for specialized platforms like Shopify. Media startups will benefit from WordPress, Ghost, or Webflow. And local brick-and-mortar businesses can choose between easy-to-use builders like Wix or Squarespace based on budget and design preferences. While custom development may sometimes be necessary to scale, using a no-code website builder is the best way for non-technical founders to launch their business without wasting time and money. Keeping things simple is key, and all options discussed can take a company with the right product and marketing strategy from zero to millions in revenue.

Invest in a Robust Internal Communications Platform

As any company grows, communication between employees and departments becomes more complicated. It might be hard to bring everyone together for in-person and online meetings. The group chat becomes a messy sequence of inside jokes and project-specific questions. Before it becomes too difficult to communicate with all staff, non-tech founders can invest in a single interface to host all internal communication. Unfortunately, choosing the right interface is not always obvious, and switching from one to another can be expensive and time consuming, and runs the risk of losing valuable information in the process.

While project management software can support a degree of communication—think Asana, Notion, or Monday—it cannot be confused with a communication platform. Communication on project management software is almost always project specific, and it is unnecessarily tedious to set up company-wide communication channels on these platforms. WhatsApp and other messaging apps might work for a while, but as a company grows, these chat apps are not ideal. Some messaging apps lack crucial features like channel organization and search, and many are not designed for sharing large documents and files. A company's communication should also remain professional, and using a work-dedicated tool helps set the right tone. What is most beneficial to a company in terms of communication is a single interface designed for optimizing communication. This narrows the options down to two ideal candidates: Slack and Discord.

Slack and Discord are two powerful platforms for optimizing a company's communication channels, but there are definite pros and cons to each depending on a company's needs. At a macro level, Slack tends to be more professional. It is easy to file and share documents, create private channels, and engage in cross-company communication.

Discord, on the other hand, got its start in the gaming community and tends to be more popular among younger generations. Many people will recognize Discord as the platform on which classified military documents were leaked. While I don't recommend sharing US government secrets on Discord, it does have file-sharing and administrator tools for regulating threads within a large online community.

Discord can host any number of audio and/or video channels and keep them running for as long as needed. While this feature was designed for gamers playing long hours together from remote locations, some companies have found creative uses for this feature. In particular, media production companies and agencies tend to appreciate Discord's screen-sharing capabilities, which rival Zoom and Google Meet. Discord is also free.

Integrating Slack or Discord into a company business will influence how the company communicates both internally and externally, so non-technical founders must not make this decision lightly. Still, it is a decision that can be made without the help of a CTO. In most cases, Slack will often be the better option, though there are nearly identical services on the horizon to watch out for, like SpiderOak's Semaphor and Keybase's Teams. For founders who are fundraising, investors are more likely to look unquestioningly on the use of Slack, while Discord may raise some eyebrows.

Communication with customers is equally important as internal communication, and there are simple tech enhancements founders can incorporate to manage customer communications as well. The best way to manage customer communication is by adopting a client relationship management (CRM) system. A good CRM system is essential for organizing your customer data, streamlining operations, building strong relationships through personalization, monitoring sales opportunities, and scaling the business. We'll discuss the various types of CRM systems, and how to select the right one for your business, in the next chapter.

Ensure Basic Security

As an entrepreneur, you are responsible for personal and customer data. Failing to keep data secure can lead to identity theft (yours or your customers), loss of trust in your business, hefty fines, and even bankruptcy. While the topic may seem scary, there are a few simple steps you can take to ensure basic security of your company's data.

Split Your Work and Personal Hardware

While it is common to use your personal phone for work purposes, there is a benefit to separating your hardware for work and personal use. At the very least, you can create two separate user accounts on your computer. This way, you will be able to split the software you use in your work life and personal life. This helps with security as well as with focus—you don't want your Netflix bookmarks on your work browser.

Choose Strong and Unique Passwords

Using the same password across accounts is a recipe for disaster. If one account is compromised, all your accounts are vulnerable. A strong password contains a mix of letters, numbers, and symbols and is not based on personal information (e.g. your mother's maiden name or your pet's name). You can use a password manager app to generate and remember complex passwords for different accounts.

Enable Two-factor Authentication Where Possible

Two-factor authentication, or 2FA, adds an extra layer of security for your accounts. In addition to entering your password, you will need to enter a code sent to your phone or an authentication app. This way, even if your password is compromised, the account remains secure. Major tech companies like Google, Facebook, and Microsoft support 2FA. Make sure to enable it for your accounts and encourage your team to do the same.

Keep Your Operating System and Software Current

Software updates often contain security patches to fix vulnerabilities that can otherwise be exploited. Enable automatic installation of updates on your computers and phones. Outdated software is an easy target for cybercriminals.

Be Cautious of Phishing Emails and Malicious Links

Phishing refers to fraudulent emails aimed at stealing personal information or downloading malware. Never click links, download attachments, or provide sensitive data in unsolicited messages. Legitimate companies don't ask for passwords or account numbers via email. When in doubt, contact the company directly instead of replying to the message.

Perform Regular Data Backups

While security measures aim to prevent breaches and data loss, there is always a possibility of ransomware attack or hardware failure wiping out your files. Plus, there is still user error to consider: you could accidentally damage your laptop or lose it, or it could be stolen. Back up business data regularly in multiple locations to prevent loss of information and lags in your business operations. The easiest way to do this is to have an external hard drive for back up along with cloud document storage like Google Drive or iCloud.

Basic security steps like using strong passwords, enabling

2FA, automatically installing updates, being cautious of phishing, and performing regular backups can go a long way in protecting your startup. Make security a priority from day one to avoid costly mistakes down the road. Staying on top of current threats and ensuring your team follows best practices will give you peace of mind that your sensitive data remains private and safe, allowing you to focus on growing your business.

You Can Go It Alone with Simple Tech

Many non-technical founders can become distracted by incorporating custom tech into their business. Founders worry they will lose their competitive advantage if they use the same tech their competitors do. A competitor can clone a business model, yes. But founders scrambling to use custom tech over simple tech forget their competitive edge is often in the intangibles—the creativity of the blog posts, the flavor of food, the quality of customer service. Custom technology won't save a company if the core offering is lacking. And simple tech can save founders time and money, which they can devote to further improving their core offering.

A tech team isn't always necessary to get a company off the ground. Moreover, it's in your best interest to accomplish as much as possible with a few hundred dollars before enlisting a tech agency for thousands of dollars. Even if an overseas development team promises to complete a project, like a website, for just a few hundred dollars, the turnaround time could be weeks, when you could have purchased simple tech and completed the project in a day. Simple tech is advantageous because it is fast, cheap, and straightforward. For ecommerce, blogging, media hosting, and most brick-and-mortar stores, simple tech is what you need to provide a strong foundation, streamline business functions, and keep the company competitive.

Chapter 3:
Automate Your
Simple Tech Platform

With the tools and services of simple tech, non-technical founders can automate and streamline many aspects of their business to take it to the next level. Think accounting automation, marketing automation, data analytics, legal form generators, and project management software. Compared to the cost of hiring employees or contractors to perform this work, the upfront cost of simple tech enhancements—particularly automation tools—pays for itself almost immediately.

Building a platform on simple tech is one job, but automating the platform and integrating different parts is another. It can be tempting to hire a developer or a tech-savvy friend or *anyone* to take care of the related work for you. I assure you that is unnecessary. Simple tech is your friend, and it's fairly easy to work with it.

The purpose of automations and integrations is to streamline your business model and operations. This means the routine tasks of your business are executed faster. There are countless automation tools available, but properly integrating them can be tricky. Fortunately, most of the tools you will need are plug-and-play, meaning you won't have to write a single line of code. We'll call these tools "simple tech enhancements." It might take a few hours to set each one up, but they will save you numerous hours in the long run.

In this chapter, we will cover a few different aspects of simple tech enhancements. First, we'll cover the various categories of enhancements. Along the way, we'll clarify some misconceptions about simple tech, specifically as it relates to the competitiveness of your business model. Then, we'll discuss how simple tech enhancements help non-technical entrepreneurs avoid miscategorizing their product type. Let's dive in…

The Types of Simple Tech Enhancements

Without the help of technology, the simplest business can demand hours of manual labor from business owners and employees. These human hours might be spent logging inventory, organizing financial records, generating lists of prospective leads, creating employee schedules, and securing sensitive client information. And that's not to mention all the time spent communicating with customers, prospective customers, employees, and business partners. An entrepreneur could spend an entire work week taking care of these chores. But with some simple tech enhancements, all of these chores can be automated, freeing up hours of time for business owners to work on executive tasks.

As an example, if you have a delivery service or an ecommerce store, you may have a complex supply chain. You may have successfully set up your site on Shopify, but still have a number of personal responsibilities: communicating with clients, procuring raw materials, customizing products, shipping finished products, and coordinating with suppliers. The conventional approach to tackling these responsibilities would be to create folders and spreadsheets to track and categorize orders and customer details. With a handful of simple tech enhancements, you can automate all of these processes.

Customer Relationship Management (CRM) Systems

As you develop your simple tech platform, you will likely create your own system for tracking data related to your customers. This often includes logging names, addresses, past orders, current orders, and details of your correspondence with them. However, as your business grows, and there are more orders and unique customers to track, keeping all of this information straight can be tedious and daunting. And entrusting new employees with the upkeep of your hand-crafted system can lead to mistakes and gaps in the data. Thankfully, client relationship management (CRM) systems exist to streamline the process of managing customer data and interactions.

For startups, choosing the right CRM system and learning to use it properly can make a world of difference in sales and customer service. Like an internal communications system, a CRM system centralizes all customer information and serves as a reference point for the whole company. All of your sales or customer service (CS) representatives can work with any customer to solve the customer's specific needs or issues. No more waiting for one sales rep to return from vacation to solve one customer's issue. Access to customer data saves CS and sales teams time, and keeps customers moving through the sales or conflict resolution pipelines.

Additionally, a CRM system saves marketing and sales teams time, effort, and money. With a CRM system, marketing and sales reps can review customer spending habits to better understand which customers to target for certain products and services. Reps might be able to recognize patterns in spending based on a specific location or demographic. For example, they may be able to recognize certain customer cohorts only spend money if they have a coupon code or deep discount.

A good CRM system centralizes all customer information in one place. It stores contacts, interactions, notes, deals, tasks, and more. You can instantly see the full history of your relationship with any customer and pick up where you left off. CRMs also allow automated workflows and reminders so that no task falls through the cracks.

The core functions of a CRM system include: contact management, scheduling, email marketing, project management, and sales pipeline visibility. However, modern CRMs integrate with many other tools to create a powerful ecosystem. You can connect your CRM system to email providers, calendar apps, accounting software, marketing automation platforms, and more. This allows data to pass between systems automatically, enabling you and your team to work in a single interface.

For example, you can set up a workflow to automatically log all Gmail emails from a deal related to a deal in your CRM system and assign follow-up tasks. You can also connect your CRM system to accounting tools like Xero or QuickBooks to automatically create invoices for clients and update payments. Some CRMs offer built-in marketing automation features, like Drip email campaigns, while others integrate with third-party systems.

There are three general types of CRM systems. The first type is a Collaborative CRM, which helps businesses internally with cross-departmental transparency related to customer information. The second type is an Operational CRM, which creates a seamless experience for users from the moment they first visit your site to the time they officially become your customer. And the third type is an Analytical CRM, which is a data-centric system that helps businesses make sense of customer behavior.

Collaborative CRM Systems

When a prospective customer interacts with a company, a number of people tend to get involved. One of the fatal flaws in pursuing these leads is internal miscommunication as various people and departments communicate with the lead. A salesperson might tell a customer the company can take care of any desired customizations, but then a project manager might not hear about the nuances until work has already begun. When these gaffes add up, the cost in time and dollars can sink budding companies with high growth potential.

A Collaborative CRM system is designed to solve such internal miscommunication problems. Companies like Salesforce, HubSpot, and SAP are well known for creating Collaborative CRM systems, but they tend to offer enterprise packages for bigger companies. Options for small to mid-sized companies include Trello, Asana, or JIRA.

Operational CRM Systems

Even if systems are working smoothly inside the company, this does not guarantee that customers are having a pleasant experience. A prospective customer may have trouble navigating the website, customizing their order, or initiating communication with the company. When these problems go unsolved, customers tend to give up and turn to competitors. And this lost business can starve a startup.

To streamline the customer-facing side of your platform, you might consider an Operational CRM. Operational CRM systems—such as Pipedrive, Zendesk, and Insightly—address everything from a customer's first click on your website to their last, including systems for customer support. Rather than manually following up with each lead, an Operational CRM system can collect site visitors' contact information, follow up with automated emails, and guide a customer through a buying process without the need for human intervention.

For example, Pipedrive specializes in sales pipeline management. It collects information about website visitors and new leads, then assigns them to the appropriate salesperson and provides reminders about when and how to follow up. The salesperson can then customize email sequences for each lead to move them through the sales funnel. For companies with long or complex sales cycles, especially B2B companies, this level of automation provides a significant competitive advantage. No lead slips through the cracks, and salespeople stay on top of their responsibilities.

Operational CRM systems can assist your business with customer support, as well. If a customer wants to speak to customer support, an Operational CRM system automatically gathers information from the customer and organizes it for you and your team to address on the backend. This means your reps might be able to solve the problem with a single email or quick phone call because they'll have all the needed information before interacting with the customer. Zendesk is a popular customer support CRM that allows you to organize support tickets, customer FAQs, and communication with customers. It provides context about each customer's history with your company so support agents can personalize their interactions.

The benefits of an Operational CRM are substantial. They allow business owners to provide customers with a seamless, personalized experience that keeps a client engaged with a company. They also help minimize wasted time and effort in managing leads and supporting customers. And Operational CRMs provide data-driven insights into how customers interact with your business so you can continue optimizing your sales and support processes.

While enterprise CRM systems may seem complex, many options for small and medium businesses are affordable, easy to set up, and integrate with the other tools in your simple tech stack. Implementing an Operational CRM could be one of the most impactful simple tech enhancements you make as you scale up your simple tech platform.

Analytical CRM Systems

The amount of data you can collect from your sales systems can be overwhelming. In fact, most companies don't end up using the majority of the data they collect from their customers. This isn't surprising when you consider the amount of time it takes to log, organize, graph, and analyze that data. That's where Analytical CRM systems come in.

Some CRM systems that work well for analytical purposes include ClickUp, Airtable, Domo, and Tableau. These tools make it easy to collect, organize, and report on large amounts of data. They are also customizable, allowing you to set up the system in a way that suits your particular business needs. While data analysis may seem complicated, Analytical CRM systems are designed to simplify the process and provide actionable results, even for those without a technical background. By learning to leverage the data you have access to, you can make better decisions, spot new opportunities, and gain an edge over your competitors.

Collaborative, Operational, and Analytical CRM systems

are all available for reasonable subscription prices, and most can easily integrate with other simple tech enhancements, too. Some systems, such as Airtable, can operate across categories—it is categorized as an Analytical CRM, but could also function as an Operational or a Collaborative CRM.

In summary, a good CRM system helps startups organize customer data, streamline operations, build strong relationships through personalization, monitor sales opportunities, uncover insights, and scale their business. The key is finding the right solution, integrating it with other tools, and using it diligently to maintain a complete and accurate customer database. Startups that get this right will be in a great position to outperform competitors.

Human Resource Management (HRM) Systems

One of the biggest obstacles and costs facing any growing business is hiring and retaining talent. A company can have a highly competitive product, a loyal customer base, and all the right customer management systems in place, but if they don't have the staffing to execute the business model then there is no business. The time it takes for business owners to interview, hire, train, and manage new employees is significant. So, costs compound when owners must hire multiple employees, employees quit, or the business needs to lay off employees.

Without a system to keep track of employee interviews, onboarding, payroll, taxes, benefits, and reviews, it's easy for founders to fall into the role of "director of human resources." They might realize they're spending more time conducting interviews and helping train new staff than they are on higher-order tasks. In particular, non-tech founders employing a lot of people benefit from a comprehensive database to manage human resources.

There are many types of HRM systems available:

• **Recruiting software** helps companies post jobs, source candidates, and manage the interview process. Popular options include Greenhouse, Lever, and JazzHR. These tools allow you to post jobs on multiple sites, track applicants, schedule interviews, and collaborate with your team when making a decision.

• **Onboarding software** helps companies manage the hiring and onboarding process. Tools like BambooHR and Namely help you extend job offers, complete background checks, set up payroll, and onboard new hires. They ensure a smooth transition for new employees joining your team.

• **Core HR software** provides comprehensive people-management tools. Solutions like Gusto, Zenefits, and People keep records of all your employees and contractors. They handle payroll, benefits, time off, employee documents, and HR compliance. These end-to-end systems are ideal for most small to mid-size companies.

• **Performance management software** helps track employee performance and development. Tools such as Reflektive and Lattice offer features for setting and tracking employee goals, sharing feedback, and running performance reviews. They help boost employee engagement and retention, too.

• **Applicant tracking systems (ATS)** help companies manage the entire recruiting process in one place. They allow you to post jobs on multiple sites, accept and review applications, schedule interviews, and make hiring decisions. Popular ATS options include SmartRecruiters, Jobvite, and Workable.

Like most of the simple tech enhancements discussed in this chapter, HRMs can take a fair amount of time to set up. However, the time you spend automating human resource tasks pays for itself tenfold. You will have more capacity to focus on your business, develop your product, and scale up instead of putting out fires. HRMs, like CRMs, are plug-and-play, and they don't require you to write a single line of code. An HRM tool is one of the most valuable simple tech enhancements an expanding company can implement.

Financial Management Systems

Few problems haunt new business owners more than a tax audit, simply because of the amount of time it takes to gather all the required financial information for the auditor. It isn't until an auditor asks for itemized revenue from all your different revenue streams, tips, expenses, overhead, and financial support for who knows how many tax quarters that most owners realize how scrambled their financial systems are. If your finances haven't been well managed, then you'll find yourself doing years of financial management work by hand on a crunched, high-stakes deadline, and often pay through the nose for it.

Most entrepreneurs don't realize they need an automated financial management system until it's too late. If all the money is going to the bank and checks go out on time, then what's the problem? End-of-year tax accountants are not too expensive and, until that time comes, it's not that hard to monitor the company's finances yourself. Many entrepreneurs actually enjoy looking at the numbers, especially when they're good. But if you're in business long enough, you need all your finances to be in order.

The reality is that financial management doesn't have to be a big deal if you set your company up with an automated financial management system. These tools can easily integrate with your business bank accounts to automatically import transactions and keep records up to date. They can also integrate with payment processors like Stripe so you can automatically reconcile payments from customers. Two good options are QuickBooks and Xero.

If you run an ecommerce store, with an automated financial management system, you can connect your Stripe account to automatically import payments and refunds. You can also connect your business bank accounts so that deposits, transfers, and other transactions flow directly into your financial management system. This means you'll have a real-time view of your cash flow and financial position without manually entering transactions or reconciling accounts.

These systems ultimately free up more of your time to focus on the business (even if you are tempted to monitor the numbers). They ensure your records are audit-ready at any point in time and may even eliminate the need for an accountant at year's end. While setting up the integrations may require some initial time and effort, the long-term benefits for managing your finances and gaining insight into the health of your business are well worth it.

Tools for Minor Improvements and AI Integrations

Sometimes a collection of minor improvements can be just as effective as one big improvement. In the old days of motorsport, racing teams only cared about the driver, the tires, and the engine. Those were the three key components that contributed to speed. But there came a day when teams realized hundreds of tiny changes to the aerodynamics of a car could improve a car's speed just as much as a better engine. The teams who took the time to make these hundreds of changes remained competitive, and the ones who neglected to make the minor improvements fell into obsolescence.

The simple tech enhancements we discussed in the previous section are big improvements you can make to streamline your business. This section will look at a number of minor improvements that, working together, can provide a comparable boost. We'll start by re-examining some tools from Chapter 2 to see how we can extend their use. Then we'll touch on some other simple tech enhancements like chatbots and eSignature tools. Lastly, we'll look at a handful of AI integrations available to simple tech platforms. Each automation will give you back a bit more time to focus on growing your business.

Chatbots

Many of us think of chatbots as annoying chat bubbles that pop up when we're casually browsing a web page. And for most users, that is exactly the case. But there will also be a handful of users genuinely interested in your product or service, and a chatbot is an easy way to start gathering information. From the user's point of view, a transaction with a chatbot may remove some of the pressure of talking to a real human. And, from your point of view, a chatbot assists a customer in initiating a transaction with zero time or energy spent on your part.

eSignature Tools

Sending paperwork back and forth for signatures is tedious and time consuming. Tools like DocuSign and HelloSign allow you to sign legally binding documents electronically.

Here's how they work: You upload your document to the eSignature service and specify where signatures are needed. You then send the document to signers through the service via email, and they can quickly and securely add their signature from any device. There's no more printing, signing, scanning, and emailing paperwork.

You can integrate eSignature tools with many of the file storage and CRM systems we've discussed. This means you can send contracts and agreements for signature directly from the tools you use every day. For example, if a customer agrees to terms in an email, you can send the contract for eSignature without losing momentum.

Using an eSignature tool is one of the simplest ways to cut down on paperwork and speed up legal processes in your business. Best of all, electronic signatures are legally valid and binding in most parts of the world. Overall, eSignature services ultimately free up more time for you to focus on high-priority tasks, instead of managing paperwork.

Scheduling Systems

Another easy way to improve efficiency in your business operations is to use an online scheduling system. Tools like Calendly, Schedulefly, and Deputy make it simple to schedule everything from meetings to classes to employee shifts.

With a scheduling system, you create different types of events—such as a 30-minute consultation or weekly classes—and the service generates a link you can share to schedule that specific calendar item. Customers or employees can then book available time slots on your calendar. The system syncs across your own calendar and your team's calendars to avoid double-booking.

Using a scheduling system means no more back-and-forth emails trying to find a time to meet. People can quickly choose what works best for them, and your calendar stays organized. These services are easy to set up and use, and many integrate directly into your existing calendar software or CRM system.

Overall, a scheduling system is an easy way to save time and provide a better experience for your customers and team. Less time spent on scheduling means more time to use solving important problems and growing your business.

AI Integrations

There are many, more complex integrations that simple tech platforms can take advantage of, and most fall under the umbrella of AI. Bloggers, for example, can pay for AI-generated images to accompany their articles, and vloggers can pay for AI-generated music for their videos instead of licensing expensive images and songs. Companies that benefit from transcribed interviews can integrate a tool like Otter.ai so that all their Zoom recordings and phone calls are automatically recorded and transcribed. Some architectural firms can make use of AI software that converts 2D renderings and blueprints into 3D models. And we're barely scratching the surface.

Even if your company is building a simple product, it would be wise to at least consider the benefits that complex technology can bring to your operations. New technology is constantly being commoditized for mass usage, and the companies that are up to speed will remain competitive. The ones that ignore technological progress will remain slow and may ultimately fail. Don't let the intangible value of your company suffer by failing to understand the enhancements—both minor and major—that can be made to your simple tech platform. Be as strategic as you can, but don't be idle.

With a variety of AI tools emerging, like GPT-4 or Google's Bard, AI integration possibilities for business spread far beyond just natural language processing or predictive analytics. I will unpack more about sophisticated AI in chapter 9. But for simple tech I like to think of easy AI integrations in three categories—language, visual, and audio. Let's explore each.

Language as an Input: ChatGPT, Bard, Anthropic's Claude

When you integrate AI into your simple tech platform, using language as input, you can begin to see efficiencies in your business—from meeting coordination to market research. Tools like ChatGPT, Bard, and Anthropic's Claude can take language as input and produce the following output:

Instant research. AI can instantly search the web and provide summarized answers to questions on any topic. This can help you gain quick insights and make better decisions without spending hours researching.

Personalized advice. AI can provide personalized advice tailored to your specific business, goals, and challenges. The advice will improve over time as AI learns more about the business and individuals involved.

Consistent brand messaging. AI can help ensure all external communications like emails, social media posts, and marketing materials have a consistent voice and message. This strengthens the company's brand without requiring manual oversight and editing of each piece of content.

Meeting preparation. AI can help you prepare for meetings by reviewing the attendee list, objectives and agenda, compiling relevant documents or reports, and suggesting discussion questions or goals. No configuration is needed to realize these benefits.

Template building. AI can help construct basic templates for documents, emails, presentations, spreadsheets, forms, and contracts to streamline repetitive work. Using a few examples or specifications, I can generate templates quickly without customization.

Market research. AI tools have access to a broad range of public data sources for instant research into markets, customers, competitors, and trends. I can start providing general market research findings and reports without any configuration. Customized research that is focused on a business's target audience may need additional info.

Idea generation. AI can instantly brainstorm relevant ideas, options, solutions, or suggestions based on a broad prompt or question from the user. No customization is needed to start ideating, though ideas may be more targeted if the AI has a deeper understanding of the business and key objectives.

Marketing copywriting. AI can generate copy for ad campaigns, eye-catching titles for blog posts, meta descriptions for a website and email subject lines. This helps ensure all marketing copy is consistent, optimized for maximum engagement, and easy to produce.

Visual-related AI

When visuals are provided as input, AI tools can offer businesses a range of services from logo generation to video editing and even interior design samples.

Image generation. AI can produce generic images, photos, or artwork to accompany blog posts, videos, social media posts, and marketing materials. This type of service is already used widely in branding. For example, you can generate your company logo with a few prompts to an image generation model. The leader in this space, at the time of writing, is Midjourney, but tools like Leonardo.ai and open source stable diffusion models are catching up.

Image editing. AI can also edit and manipulate images. For example, it can remove objects, fill empty areas, and apply different aesthetic styles. Recent improvements have been made in the image upscaling field. For example, AI can create a full 4k version of a small image.

Video editing. AI can edit raw video footage by splitting clips, adding transitions, inserting titles or graphics, stabilizing shaky footage, and color correcting. For example, you can generate TikTok videos from one YouTube video with a click of a button. Traditional video editing software like Adobe's Premiere Pro also have AI add-ons to reduce time spent editing.

3D modeling. AI can generate 3D models, renderings, or animations from 2D designs, sketches, photos, scans, or other visual data. Significant customization and examples are typically required for AI to understand a company's particular needs and branding in 3D.

Visual styling or design. AI can generate visual styles, themes, templates, or full design concepts for a company's website, app, product, marketing materials, and social media profiles. Lately, I've been impressed by developments in interior design generation via text. For example, I discovered a Ukrainian home design brand that uses AI to generate tons of beautiful mock interiors, including details like folklore ornaments and natural embedding of color and furniture in rendered homes. Fascinating!

Audio-related AI

Audio inputs allow AI to enhance your business in myriad practical and creative ways.

Transcription. AI can automatically transcribe audio from phone calls, video conferences, interviews, and podcasts into text. This helps make the information more accessible for searching and analyzing. Many transcription services like Temi, Rev, and Otter are available to integrate into simple tech platforms. Some services are better than others, so if you're using transcripts for ADA (American Disabilities Act) compliance purposes, double check the transcription services's accuracy.

Voice cloning. AI can generate synthetic voices that match a particular speaker's voice using samples of their speech. This could allow for automated voice responses, interactive voice messaging, or other applications where a human voice is preferred but not always available. Significant customization and data are required for effective voice cloning.

Audio editing. Similar to video editing, AI can edit and manipulate raw audio files by removing background noise, applying filters or effects, rearranging sections, and adjusting levels. This can help produce higher quality audio content and podcasts in less time. AI audio editing tools may require some customization and examples to understand a user's needs.

Audio styling or sound design. For some types of media or products, AI could potentially generate custom audio styles, sound designs, sound effects, or full soundtracks and scores. Significant customization and examples would be needed for AI to develop an understanding of the appropriate audio styling for a particular business or brand. The quality may still not match that of a human sound designer.

Music generation. AI can generate short original music clips or full compositions in a particular style or genre based on a text or audio prompt. The quality and applicability of AI-generated music may not yet match that of human composers and would likely require additional editing or customization. However, it blows my mind how far this technology has come. AI-generated songs are good enough to put into your background in a podcast or YouTube video.

AI for Workflow Automation, or Connecting the Dots

The goal of workflow automation is to reduce time spent on repetitive tasks by automating them, where possible. At Aleph One, for example, every time a potential client schedules a meeting on our website, they are automatically sent an extended questionnaire to better prepare for the meeting. The client can submit their pitch deck and answer more questions about their industry, their tech, their audience, and their goals. Once the questionnaire is completed, the calendar invite is updated to include the information. This way, anyone who will be joining the meeting has enough information to adequately prepare. This is just one example, but modern automation tools follow this same simple logic of multistep workflows.

Workflow automation tools usually have triggers and actions. A *trigger* could be any event happening with any digital tool—an incoming email, a new message in Slack, a task updated in Asana, a new post on a specific website. Modern tools have thousands of possible trigger events. *Actions* are done by one of those tools, like sending an email, changing the status of a blog post, updating a task in a CRM system, or sending a mobile notification. There are more actions available than most people can imagine.

At Aleph One, we use tools like Zapier, make.com, and IFTTT to automate our processes as much as possible. One of our most complex automation flows is in content writing for our blog. When a new question is posted on Reddit or Quora by startup founders, we send it to GPT-4 to generate ideas for a blog post. We then record the ideas using Airtable. Every morning, I go over the newly generated ideas for blog posts and extract a couple ideas we can actually work on. For the ideas I like, I change the status to "Ready for AI." It is then sent to our AI workflow, which proceeds as follows:

1. GPT-4 receives and then analyzes 10 articles on the topic from a Google search, providing a critique for each article.

2. GPT-4 offers ideas for the structure of a unique blog

post, in order to create the best content on this topic given existing content and critiques.

3. The automated workflow sends the GPT-4 outputs back to Airtable for me to pick up, changing the status of the article to "Ready for structure review." I can see the proposed article structure and some content from the internet.

4. I change the article structure to make sure we are actually providing value and insights, drawing on our experience working with startups. I then change the article status to "Ready for Writer."

5. The writer fills in the article based on the drafted structure, and changes the status to "Ready for Marketing Copy AI."

6. The article is then picked up by GPT-4, generating an SEO-friendly article title, meta tags, Twitter copy, and LinkedIn copy. This copy is sent back to Airtable, and the status of the article is changed to "Ready for Publishing."

7. Finally, the article is sent to our automated content calendar with automated post publishing to all our social media accounts and our blog.

With this workflow, we have a consistent flow of ideas for our blog, and we save tons of time. Most of my time is spent on reviewing ideas and putting in crucial industry expertise to make the content worth reading. This is one example of what is possible with AI-assisted workflow automation, but you could think broader—beyond content production to marketing process, sales, operations, and customer success.

Avoid Miscategorizing Your Product with Simple Tech Enhancements

It's important to understand that simple tech enhancements can be applied to all three product types—Simple, Custom, and Wild. These enhancements can streamline your business operations and improve efficiency, but they don't necessarily change the fundamental nature of your product. In other words, integrating simple tech enhancements doesn't automatically transform a Simple product into a Custom or Wild one.

Everything we've discussed so far in terms of simple tech enhancements can be achieved without the need for a CTO or a tech partner. These plug-and-play tools are designed to be accessible and user-friendly, even for non-technical entrepreneurs. By leveraging these tools, you can optimize your business operations and stay competitive in the market.

As companies scale, enhancements and even custom solutions are often necessary to support growth. You would be remiss not to leverage simple tech for as long as possible before transitioning to custom development. Doing so will allow more time to focus on perfecting the product, marketing, and customer experience—the real drivers of success.

Now, strengthening the competitiveness and defensibility of your product signals you're entering the realms of Custom and Wild. This is when you start doing things with your technology and your business model that nobody else is doing.

When you start deviating from simple tech and can still prove the efficacy of your platform—meaning the increase in your margins makes up for the increase in your tech expenses—then the added value to your company is tangible. Before you take this leap, you need to be aware of all the additional responsibilities (and risks) of Custom or Wild products. Rather, you don't need to know this, but your *tech partner* does.

Chapter 4:
CTO Responsibilities and the CTO Landscape

If your product enters the arena of Custom Tech, you will want to recruit a CTO. You don't need a CTO to get a Simple product off the ground, and a Wild product is an entirely different category (which we'll look at later). Custom products, though, require you to partner with someone who can take on CTO responsibilities.

Before looking at the landscape of potential CTOs, it is imperative you understand the responsibilities of this position. When we talk about CTO responsibilities, we are referring to six major categories of managerial expertise: technical strategy, platform architecture, intellectual property rights, phasing, team building, and managing the technology budget. A CTO's approach to these areas of management can make or break your company.

While the details of these responsibilities might sound complicated, it's not your job to fulfill them. Rather, it is your job to find someone who can. First, we'll cover the six primary responsibilities of a CTO. Then, we'll look at how to find someone who fits the mold.

Designing Technical Strategy

The first responsibility of a CTO is to design a technical strategy, which is how technology impacts your business model or business case. Technical strategy goes beyond your company's ability to integrate and build competitive technology. It must also consider current technological innovations in your industry, and in related industries, which could affect your competitiveness.

When developing a technical strategy for your company, your CTO must understand how your technical capabilities affect your platform, development, and products. He must consider how consumers interact with your product, how changes in one area of development affect another, and how the product performs as a whole. It is a constant juggling act to keep all your company's technology working together seamlessly as your tech team works to improve and scale it.

As an example, consider the tribulations of Jet, an ecommerce company that began in 2016. Jet launched with a promise to offer lower prices than Amazon and Walmart. Jet's business model depended on maintaining minimal margins, at times even selling products below cost. However, Jet did not have the technical capabilities to execute this model and remain profitable.

Specifically, Jet lacked strong technology for pricing optimization, supply chain management, and fraud prevention. Its systems could not monitor competitors' pricing in real-time to ensure it was the lowest, nor could it determine optimal pricing for the thousands of products it offered. As a result, Jet often over discounted and lost money on sales.

Jet also lacked the technical integrations to efficiently match customer demand with supplier inventory across its millions of items. It wound up placing large orders from suppliers to avoid stockouts, but then faced overstock of slow-moving goods. The excess inventory added substantial costs. Finally, Jet's limited fraud detection technology left it exposed to illicit activity like credit card fraud, coupon abuse, and product return fraud. These problems alone cost Jet tens of millions in losses per year.

To resolve these technical issues, Jet had to invest heavily in building machine learning models, data pipelines, and other technologies to solve its pricing, supply chain, and fraud problems. After three years, and losing over $100 million, Jet was finally acquired by Walmart, who could provide the technical might Jet lacked.

With more robust technology in place from the start, Jet could have avoided the massive losses that nearly doomed its business. Strong technical strategy is critical even for startups in non-technical fields. Jet serves as a cautionary tale of the importance of aligning technical capabilities with the business model.

As another example, the rise and fall of Quibi highlights the importance of balancing tech strategy with customer behavior and wants. In 2020, Quibi launched as a mobile-only video streaming service focused on short-form content. The company shut down just six months after launch, despite raising $1.75 billion in funding from major Hollywood studios and tech investors. It was a remarkably fast failure for a company with so many resources.

A big reason for Quibi's downfall was its technical strategy, which did not align with how audiences consume video content. Quibi invested heavily to engineer its platform around a phone-centric experience, including technology to seamlessly transition its videos between landscape and portrait mode based on how a user might hold their phone. The tech strategy assumed that short-form video optimized for mobile phones would resonate with younger viewers and offer new opportunities for streaming services. However, data on viewing habits clearly showed that the vast majority of streaming took place on TVs, not phones. Creating content exclusively for streaming on a mobile device proved unappealing to most audiences.

If Quibi had paid attention to the research on viewing preferences and behaviors of its target audience, it would have realized a mobile-only streaming service was doomed to fail. With a more data-driven technical strategy, Quibi could have adapted its content and platform to support mobile *and* TV viewing, and saved resources by foregoing less important technology like landscape-portrait transitions. This would have given the streaming service a much better chance at gaining traction with viewers, and therefore a shot at business sustainability.

Quibi serves as another cautionary tale of how poor technical strategies can lead startups to waste money and effort on ideas that have little chance of working. When launching an innovative new service, it is critical to develop a technical roadmap grounded in *facts about customer needs and preferences*. Without this data-driven approach, even the most well-funded companies can quickly fail.

These two examples together demonstrate the many considerations and challenges a CTO must navigate when designing a technical strategy. The technical strategy entails several key components that the CTO is responsible for developing and implementing. Being responsible for your business's technology strategy means being responsible for the following components:

Choosing the right technology stack. This includes programming languages, frameworks, databases, and cloud providers. The makeup of a tech stack depends on product requirements, team expertise, cost, scalability, and other factors. A good CTO evaluates options and makes an informed decision.

Platform architecture. The CTO oversees the product's overall software architecture, ensuring different components work together seamlessly and the product can scale as needed. This includes principles of modularity, redundancy, high availability, fault tolerance, and more.

Integration with third parties. Many products integrate with payment providers, analytics tools, email services, and other third parties. The CTO ensures these integrations work reliably and securely.

Security strategy. The CTO develops approaches to application security, data security, identity and access management, and other aspects of cybersecurity. Having a thoughtful and proactive security strategy is critical for any customer-facing product.

Technology roadmap. The CTO outlines a high-level roadmap of how the product will evolve technically to gain a competitive advantage, including plans for new features, scaling, performance improvements, and more. The roadmap needs to align with the overall product and business strategy.

Staying up to date with innovations. A good CTO continuously monitors trends in software engineering, cloud computing, open-source projects, and other areas of technology. They understand how new tools and techniques can benefit the product, and they will take action to incorporate them when it makes sense.

Technical debt management. All products accumulate technical debt over time—the CTO ensures this debt doesn't get out of control. The CTO has a plan to refactor code, upgrade dependencies, containerize applications, and take other measures to improve quality and flexibility of the codebase.

Developing and implementing a company's technical strategy, in and of itself, could be considered a full-time job, and while important, it is only one-fifth of the CTO's responsibilities.

Designing Platform Architecture

The second responsibility of your CTO is to design platform architecture, which entails choosing the technologies your company can use to build your software. Part of planning your platform's architecture is a matter of preference. Your CTO may be more proficient in one area of code than another (although, ideally, they have some knowledge of several coding languages—more on that later). One coding language might be better suited for the type of product you're building, whether it be related to audio-visual media, data analysis, or financial technology.

However, language preference is just one factor that a CTO must consider when planning a platform's architecture. Choosing the right cloud provider is another preference. If your CTO has expertise with only one cloud provider, that doesn't mean it is the best fit for the project.

A crucial part of designing platform architecture is selecting a programming language. Even though complex projects may involve the use of multiple programming languages, successful companies select a primary language that best aligns with the specific needs and goals of company projects or products. And the type of architecture you use is often the biggest factor in your company's security—which is a big consideration if you plan to collect and store customer data.

Designing platform architecture also involves legal compliance. If you're a FinTech startup, there are data protection laws your platform must comply with, and you can expect an audit before even going live. For example, you must be compliant in the way you store personal financial data coming from third-party integrations, such as Plaid (a banking data provider). Worst case scenario is you build your platform, get audited, and the audit determines you don't comply with security standards. Your team will have to rework the parts which did not pass the audit or start from scratch.

Integration is another factor when designing platform architecture. Often, when you integrate with other platforms, those platforms must also pass a security assessment and analysis. Every time you look to develop your platform or integrate another platform, your CTO must consider how the change will affect all the other areas of your company's tech as well as your security compliance.

When designing platform architecture, your CTO must ask questions like:

- Is the chosen technology stack scalable and future-proof?
- Where are the weak spots in our current architecture?
- What might be weak points in future architecture?
- What is the learning curve for our development team to adopt the new chosen technology stack? How can our architecture be improved for smoother development?
- Will these changes to our platform make it harder to integrate with other platforms?
- How easy is it to maintain and update the

architecture?

- Will the architecture pass security standards?

Answering these questions requires an extensive awareness of technology and software architecture beyond the scope of your company, which is an important consideration to keep in mind when approaching CTO candidates.

Managing Intellectual Property Rights

The third responsibility of the CTO is managing the intellectual property (IP) rights of the company's tech. This might sound like the responsibility of a lawyer, but most lawyers can't read two sets of code and understand why one breaks IP law and the other passes. It falls on your CTO to understand which code belongs to someone else, and which code your company is innovating (so that you can patent and protect it).

Managing IP rights is easy to treat as peripheral, but when it comes to technical IP there are millions of dollars at stake. If your company tries to spin off third-party code as its own and that third party sues you, how do you know you'll be able to defend your case? If your CTO wasn't careful to record the unique modifications your company made to the code, you can lose the ability to use certain code in your application and pay a hefty legal penalty.

It is the CTO's job to be aware of all the patents you might be brushing up against as you develop and integrate technology. This is especially necessary when you partner with other tech agencies. An agency might say they have code that can fulfill your needs, but where did that code come from? Did they write that code? Or did they spin it off from another company's code? You don't get a free pass for violating a patent just because you didn't know you were violating it. Someone must be on the lookout, finding what the potential patent violations are, and working to avoid them before they happen.

High-profile examples of closely guarded IP are numerous and include the following:

- **Netflix's recommendation algorithm.** Netflix's movie recommendation algorithm, which they call Cinematch, has been key to their success. They have not patented the algorithm, but they have kept the details private as a trade secret to avoid copying. Reverse engineering the algorithm would be very difficult, which helps Netflix maintain competitive advantage.

- **Google's PageRank algorithm.** Google's search algorithm, PageRank, was critical to their early success. They patented the algorithm to prevent competitors from copying it. The patent has since expired, but while active it gave Google a competitive advantage and helped establish them as the dominant search engine.

- **The *New York Times* paywall algorithm.** The *New York Times* spent significant resources developing an algorithm to determine how many free articles each reader gets before hitting a paywall. They have kept the algorithm details private to avoid copying and to maintain their competitive advantage. The paywall and associated algorithm have contributed to their financial success in the digital media industry.

There is no mercy when it comes to technical IP. Entire business models depend on the protection of patents. The biggest tech companies are constantly settling lawsuits for hundreds of millions (and in some cases billions) of dollars because they are finding evidence of their patented software in their competitors' devices. Apple and Samsung are constantly suing each other for patent violations. SAP and Oracle are constantly suing smaller tech companies for spinning off software that was only leased to them.

Here are some preventative, and also defensive, strategies your CTO should be aware of for protecting the IP your company is developing:

- **Code scanning:** Using automated tools to scan through the company's codebase and compare it against a database of open source and third-party libraries to look for unauthorized use of code. Some popular code-scanning tools include Black Duck, Veracode, and Synopsys. These tools can detect if open-source libraries are out of date or being used improperly.

- **Manual code audits:** Having engineers manually review sections of the codebase to look for potential IP issues. This is more time-consuming but can find issues that automated tools may miss. Manual audits are especially important for core areas of the code (i.e., code that is foundational to your Custom Tech).

- **Monitoring competitor products:** Analyzing the features and functionality of competitors' products to determine if they are potentially violating the company's IP. If any infringement is detected, the company can take legal action to defend their IP. However, reverse engineering competitor products also comes with risks around IP exposure, so it must be done carefully.

- **Defensive publications:** Publishing details about the company's IP, software architecture, and algorithms to establish priority. White papers are a good example. Published details make it more difficult for competitors or patent trolls to claim infringement on overly broad patents. The published details are still kept at a high level to avoid giving away trade secrets but can help protect the company legally.

- **Employee agreements:** Requiring all employees and contractors to sign IP assignment and confidentiality agreements to establish clear ownership over any work done on behalf of the company. These agreements are important in case employees leave and join a competitor or if code leaks outside the company.

You usually don't have the chance to patent your technology until you enter the Wild category, but sometimes early opportunities arise. If your CTO is on the lookout, not only will you avoid violating other companies' IP rights, but you can also jump on the chance to establish your own IP rights.

Managing Phasing

The fourth responsibility of your CTO is to manage the phases of new product development. This is where your CTO's expertise must extend beyond technical know-how and into leadership and business strategy. There are always technical considerations when creating a timeline for a product's development, but there are also business priorities. Your HR department needs to know when to hire new people. Your marketing department needs to know when to launch campaigns. And your investors need to know how soon they can see a return on their investment. It will often fall on the CTO to provide realistic expectations, based on the phases of a product's development.

A common misconception is that a CTO sets a phasing plan and never veers from it. The reality is that the phasing of products is dynamic. There should be an ongoing dialogue between you, your CTO, and your entire team regarding the phasing of products. Successful growth is not determined by how well your company sticks to an original plan, but how well your company pivots as circumstances change.

Few companies demonstrate the long-term benefits of dynamic tech phasing better than Tesla. Most people consider Tesla to be an electric car manufacturing company, but at its core the company is a tech company. The car is Tesla's product, just as the iPhone is Apple's product. There is the car as a physical object, but the value of the car is in its technology. Tesla's tech is valuable because of the ability to continue updating software after the customer purchases the product. Just as iPhones have regular software updates, so do Tesla's cars. The company has strategized phases for its software to continue developing long after customers make an initial purchase. With this kind of phasing, a Tesla can become safer, faster, and more user friendly each year. No other car on the market retains its value like a Tesla, and this is because of its technology.

When your CTO sets the phases for a product, they must ask questions like:

- **What does our product need to accomplish in the short, mid, and long term?**
- **What are the crucial business timelines, events, and milestones that might influence fundraising and forming partnerships?**
- **How can I align short-term business goals with long-term technical strategy?**
- **What are the implications of each phase regarding our ability to hire more developers, integrate new technology, and grow our profit margins?**
- **What technical debt will each phase accrue and how will we pay it off?** Technical debt refers to suboptimal code and technical decisions made to achieve short-term goals. Each phase should account for resolving technical debt to avoid long-term problems.
- **What resources do we have access to for each phase?** Resources include funding, talent, partnerships, technology, data, etc. Phasing should fit within current resource constraints, and your CTO should consider how to gain more resources for future phases.
- **How risky is each phase and what are the contingency plans?** Risk assessment and mitigation strategies

are necessary for any product roadmap. CTOs must determine acceptable levels of risk for each phase and have backup plans in case things go wrong.

- **What is the opportunity cost of each phase?** Opportunity cost refers to what you give up by choosing one phase over another. CTOs must weigh the pros and cons of each phase to determine the lowest opportunity cost and highest return on investment.

- **How will company culture and team dynamics influence the phasing?** Company culture and team dynamics have a significant impact on product development. CTOs must choose phases that play to the strengths of the team and support a healthy company culture. For example, pushing your team to its breaking point works just as many times as you take the whole team for a vacation in Thailand.

If your CTO cannot balance the business priorities with technical strategy, they will struggle to phase product development in a way that sustains long-term growth. This is why your CTO must possess both business and leadership skills plus technical skills.

Fostering Team Building

The fifth responsibility of the CTO is to foster team building. This refers to their ability to hire the right people at the right time, connect with contractors and agencies when appropriate, and evolve the team as technical strategy changes. For many

CTOs this is the most exciting part of the job, but if mishandled it can bring a company to a slow, painful death. Overhead costs will almost always be a startup's biggest expense. A CTO must be able to balance the cost of each new team member with the value they add.

There are a hundred different types of developers to choose from—desktop developers, system developers, mobile app developers, hardware integrators, developers for programming chips, web developers—and an eager CTO will want to hire all of them. They must resist this urge.

In general, there are two ways to build a tech team: with specialists and with generalists. There are a lot of specialists in the tech world who can bring incredible value to your company if the perfect job exists for them. For products in the Wild category, you may need people who specialize in blockchain, or machine learning, or FinTech, in order to build the technology in the right way. Even when building Custom products, it's tempting to hire a team of specialists. For most tech startups, though, specialists tend to hamper growth rather than aid it.

In reality, the best tech teams are the smallest ones with the widest scope of capabilities. In the long run, a team of two to six technical engineers can accomplish a lot more and in a shorter amount of time. There are a number of reasons for this. A small team of engineers can communicate faster, problem solve with more transparency, and adapt their roles to fit the company's most urgent technical needs.

At my company Aleph One, for example, the majority of our engineers are full stack who are well-versed in JavaScript and React. They can all complete both frontend and backend tasks. JavaScript is also excellent when it comes to cross-platform capabilities—we can pull off custom apps for mobile and desktop devices. And when we need to swap engineers between teams, it is easy to do so because they all have overlapping skill sets, differing only slightly in experience.

If we introduce just one specialization—say, frontend and backend split—a team becomes harder to manage. Let's say you have a backend engineer with ten years of experience, yet the majority of the tasks for a project are on the frontend. Not optimal, right? Even if your CTO keeps the backend engineer busy with tasks like fixing tech debt, the talents and salary of the experienced engineer are wasted.

In any situation, but especially in the beginning, avoid hiring specialized roles. Managed properly by the CTO, your tech team's efficiency can be maximized with a minimal overhead salary cost.

Regarding team building, your CTO must consider questions such as:

- What must my team look like for this project to successfully kick off?
- What skills are required?
- How will we handle shifting workloads?
- Are the engineers' skills cross-functional?
- How will the team need to change at different phases of the project?
- Can the same people adapt their roles, or will certain phases require a specialist?

- What does the job market look like for compiling this team?

Managing the Technology Budget

The sixth and final responsibility of a CTO, which is crucial but often underappreciated, is managing the technology budget. Creating and overseeing budgets may not sound exciting, but it is essential for achieving key product and infrastructure milestones. For startups, budgeting connects the vision for technology and growth with the resources to make it happen.

When developing technology budgets, CTOs must consider both short-term and long-term needs. In the short term, budgets must account for immediate priorities like software licenses, cloud services, new engineering hires, and product developments. CTOs must determine how to maximize limited funds by making difficult trade-offs, and they frequently need to make a persuasive case to executives for adequate budget allocations. Optimizing spending and reducing inefficiencies are also important for the financial health of a young company.

From a long-term perspective, CTOs are responsible for budgeting in a way that enables multi-year technology and product strategies. Major infrastructure overhauls, platform changes, new product features, and other large-scale initiatives must have funding mapped out well in advance. Technology roadmaps are meaningless without the budget to implement them. However, budgets also need flexibility to account for shifts in business priorities or other unforeseen changes. CTOs sit at the intersection of strategic vision and financial reality.

Managing technology budgets also requires appropriate financial controls and oversight. CTOs implement systems to monitor budgets, track spending, verify proper allocation of funds, and avoid waste or overages. They establish account-ability across their teams to ensure all members understand the role they play in resource planning and management.

For startups, securing adequate funding for technology and product needs is no easy task. Yet it is the CTO's responsibility to make a compelling case to investors and executives that the budget being requested is essential and that every dollar will be maximized. Developing budgets that balance short-term realities with long-term ambitions, and that adapt to shifts in priorities or resources, is challenging but necessary work. When done well, strong financial management and oversight allow CTOs to achieve product milestones and fuel company growth even under tight constraints. Budgeting may not be exciting, but for startups it means the difference between plans and progress.

Scaling CTO Responsibilities from Scratch

As you consider the responsibilities of a CTO, it helps to re-member that bringing on a CTO is not an urgent matter. This might sound ridiculous. After reading about their many re-sponsibilities, you may think, "I need two CTOs! I might even need three!" But the funny reality is that, *as your company is getting started*, there isn't much work for a CTO.

At a startup, a good CTO can design tech strategy, design platform architecture, phase product development, and plan a team in a couple weeks. The last thing you want to do is pay someone to tell you, "You need to license this software from this company and think about building out the customer purchasing interface with web developers and marketers." That work could take six months to a year! There's no reason to be paying someone a six-figure salary for that bit of advice. It's only when your company *takes off* that the responsibilities of a CTO become a full-time job.

Let me repeat that: you don't need to hire a CTO right away! Instead, *take time* to find the right one because it is difficult to fire a CTO if you realize they're too specialized to build a dynamic architecture and phasing strategy. When you hire someone as a CTO, you aren't just giving them a job title, but also equity in your company—sometimes double digits depending on the person.

So, how do you begin your search for a prospective CTO?

The CTO Landscape

The CTO landscape refers to the sphere of people and agencies you can realistically consider for fulfilling the CTO responsibilities at your startup. The landscape consists of four camps and, while two are far preferable than the others, all are sources for CTOs. The camps are friends, engineers, development agencies, and venture studios. It is worth noting that if your company is building a Wild product, then hiring a development agency or a developer to later grow into a CTO is not an option. But for startups building Custom products, all four camps are on the table.

Friends

The first camp to consider for your future CTO is the most intuitive option: friends. One of the biggest considerations in this process is your *level of trust* in the individual you're considering as a CTO. You need to trust your CTO, and when you partner with a friend, a friend's friend, or a friend of a friend, an organic level of trust is already established.

As an entrepreneur, you know how hard it is to build a startup. You are intimately aware of the time commitment, the strain on relationships, and the juggling of responsibilities. And if there is an upside to your struggle, it may not be for five to ten years. So, when you partner with someone as a prospective CTO, you need a high degree of certainty that when the times get tough, your CTO will be willing to work through the trials and tribulations with you.

The importance of trust cannot be overstated. When you're starting a company, you need people you can trust, especially when it comes to Custom Tech. As you've seen, the technical responsibilities can stack up quickly, and difficult decisions will need to be made while balancing product development needs and business strategy. If you don't trust your CTO, then you can't trust your business strategy will be properly executed.

In trying times, it's naturally easier to trust someone from your friend circle as compared to a developer from Upwork or an agency. This is why the first thing most entrepreneurs do when they are ready to innovate their product is say to their friend circle, "Hey, I need a tech-savvy person or connection to help me with this." If the right person pops up and is willing to help—at low cost or for free—then celebrate your miracle! But the odds are the first person to raise their hand is not the best fit to be your CTO.

There are likely *several* people you can think of who have technical experience and who would jump at the opportunity to be a part of a startup. They might even make a case for themselves by reciting their resume. "I've worked at Google... Oracle...Blizzard. I can totally develop what you have in mind!" The problem is high-profile technical experience alone is not a game changer, and there are two reasons for this. The first reason is that in bigger companies, engineers tend to have narrower—or more specific—tech experience. They're responsible for a small portion of a big enterprise. The second reason is that most tech people rarely have leadership experience.

The reality is the CTO landscape is small. Those who have broad technical expertise *and* experience managing a team are few. So, while there may be several developers in your circle who are eager to be the Steve Wozniak to your Steve Jobs, the likelihood is that they are specialized developers who are overconfident in their abilities. Most developers become like hammers—they have one job and they do it very well. However, developers often think every problem can be solved in the same way. To a hammer everything is a nail because that's the only job it knows how to do. Startups, though, encounter complicated problems that require varied experience and skills.

Even a developer with 10 years of technical experience isn't guaranteed to have the necessary leadership experience to help guide the development of your product. And if they cannot onboard and lead the right people, you're screwed. At some point you *will* need a developer but, as we'll see, very few developers have CTO potential. The risk in picking a CTO candidate out of your friend circle is that you will end up with, well, a developer.

To help you whittle down the list of potential CTO candidates, I offer this simple "HIT-3-OUT-OF-5" checklist:

1. Senior software engineering experience
2. Product architecture experience
3. Team leadership experience
4. Project management experience
5. Previous (successful) CTO experience

The magic of this checklist is that, with the exception of item five, two items are highly responsible engineering roles and two are people roles. Check off three items and you're good to go.

In summary, if you are talking to a friend who is tech savvy, but who has never had any managerial, architectural, or leadership responsibilities, they're not going to be a good CTO. The best-case scenario is that you have a friend who does in fact have managerial experience *and* technical savvy, and they are excited enough about your idea to help you build from the ground up for little or no cost. Of course, this is on the promise that there is equity and upside in the coming years.

The odds of finding a capable CTO from your friend circle are small, but not impossible, so this is the best place to start your search in the CTO landscape. If (or when) your search turns up no viable candidates, you'll have to brave one of three alternatives.

Engineers

The second camp to consider in the CTO landscape is made up of individual engineers. Hiring an engineer to grow into the CTO role, or simply to develop your product, is very common. The pros are that you have more control over who you bring on, you can evaluate their skills and fit, and, if it doesn't work out, you can let them go. The cons are: the role of CTO requires skills and experience beyond just engineering; and it can be difficult to assess whether an engineer has the chops to become a CTO.

There are a few types of engineers to consider:

- **Junior engineer:** Fresh out of college or bootcamp. Possesses basic technical skills but lacks experience. A gamble to hire, but often willing to work for less. Invest heavily in their growth but understand they may not develop into a CTO.
- **Mid-level engineer:** 3-5 years of experience. Sharpened skills and may have expertise in a particular area like frontend, backend, or DevOps. Less risky to hire but may still not develop CTO potential. Carefully evaluate their skills, experience, and fit.

- **Senior engineer:** Over 5 years of experience, usually at larger companies. Well-developed skills and may have had leadership opportunities. Less risky hires but more expensive. Evaluate skills, fit, and desire for leadership. Content to remain an engineer may not make a good CTO.

Engineers from elite companies like Google, Facebook, and Netflix are attractive but be wary of hiring for brand name alone. Pedigree does not guarantee skills or leadership ability. An engineer from a top company may expect a large salary and equity, while lacking the chops to be a CTO.

Technical skills matter, but soft skills and mindset must also be evaluated. Look for qualities like problem solving, communication, leadership potential, and a growth mindset. Ask about their aspirations and how they stay up to date with technology. Assess their drive and vision to become a CTO, not just an engineer.

A common mistake many founders make when seeking a CTO is to bypass their network of engineers and find the first developer with specialized expertise to build their product. The difference between an engineer and a developer is that engineers are responsible for systems, while developers focus on hands-on building. Hundreds of developers will jump at the chance to code your product in hopes of becoming CTO. But keep in mind—they want to *build*, not handle higher-level CTO responsibilities like blueprints, planning, strategizing, and accommodating other departments. What you want is someone with a base level of technical expertise but who has recently been in management roles.

In summary, engineers are a mixed bag in the CTO landscape. Junior engineers are risky and may not develop CTO potential, while senior engineers from top companies are attractive yet often lacking managerial experience. The ideal hire is a mid-level or senior engineer with well-developed skills and leadership ability, as well as the drive to become a CTO. However, finding this combination is challenging. If you hire an engineer, invest in their growth, but understand they still may not become your CTO. You may need to continue searching for the right candidate.

Development Agencies

The third camp in the CTO landscape is a development (dev) agency. There are tons of different agencies that offer various services. No matter which agency you choose, you will likely end up with a stable product.

If you work with a dev agency, they will iterate on a product with you until it is more or less stable by a certain due date. This creates predictability in terms of cost and timeline. The problem with agencies, as the boys at SWAG.com found out, is that they operate like mercenaries.

When you hire a mercenary, there is an immediate conflict of interest. Agencies don't care about your business strategy the way you do. You have a vision for the growth of your company. The agency has a checklist, a deadline, and a vague benchmark for making you happy. They don't get paid to tell you if a product can sustain a business or not—they get paid to create it.

That being said, most agencies will still think about technical strategy. They will think about platform architecture, IP rights, team building, and phasing to some extent. They are aware of the responsibilities of a CTO. But, unlike a CTO, they are not on the same side of the table as you. They have their own business to think about. It's in their best interest for engagements to be longer and more expensive, while you're seeking quick and inexpensive product delivery.

In summary, if you can manage the conflict of interest with an agency, they are a viable option for executing the responsibilities of a CTO. If anything, they can at least help you get an MVP off the ground. We'll discuss dev agencies in more detail in Chapter 6, in the context of growing your tech team as you phase your MVP. There is one more camp that, if successfully managed, could be your best option.

Venture Studios

Okay, full disclosure: I run a venture studio. My honest opinion, though, is that venture studios are your best option next to hiring a CTO out of your friend circle. A venture studio is a dev agency that eliminates the mercenary-esque conflict of interest by doubling as an investor. At present, these types of agencies are rare (one in a hundred, maybe), but the few that would engage in this type of partnership are worth considering.

My company, Aleph One, is this type of agency. We might be one of the few agencies that operates both as investor and as a dev agency, but I believe that venture studios will be an increasingly appealing option for startups looking to recruit CTOs. There are a few reasons I believe this. The first is that, even though Aleph One started as an average dev agency and stumbled into investment by accident, our portfolio companies grow quicker than others. It won't be long before other dev agencies recognize the benefits and seize opportunities to fill the role of CTO and reap venture capital rewards for startups.

The second reason I think venture studios will gain more traction among startups is that getting a dev agency to double as an investor reintroduces trust into the partnership. When you take investment money from a venture dev agency, they are quite literally invested in your company's success. Instead of the mercenary attitude of a standard dev agency, you can feel assured a venture dev agency will work efficiently and help guide your product(s) in a sustainable direction. They trust your company will produce a nice ROI, and you can trust them to help your company grow competitively.

Of course, there are a few pitfalls to be aware of with such a partnership. The first is that, in order for the investment to be set up well, the venture studio must invest cash (capital) in your company. There are studios out there that will offer to invest *sweat equity*, meaning they will put in human hours without pay because they believe the profit on equity will make up for the short-term sacrifice. This might sound great, but it is actually bad for business.

When a venture studio invests sweat equity, they lose money in the short term. This means there is a high likelihood their employees are underpaid, which allows them to run slim for a while. And if employees aren't paid well, they tend to leave (or if they don't leave, they certainly don't perform well). Poor performance and high turnover make sustaining business growth difficult. As a result, sweat equity is tenuous and risky. Cash investments, or no deal.

The second pitfall to be aware of when partnering with venture studios is that you are not in control of the studio's resources. The studio can say they have an all-star tech team, but you will need to ask the studio how they treat their team. It's tempting to turn a blind eye to how a venture studio treats their employees, however, because they are investing in you, you can hold the venture studio to the same employee practices.

Point blank ask the venture studio about how they treat their employees. Inquire about pay, time off, and project load. Are the engineers, developers, and coders the studio assigns to your product on several other projects at once? What sort of salary and benefits do the studio employees receive? What's the employee turnover? If the venture studio's employees are overloaded or burned out, the team's outputs will reflect this, and your product will be subpar.

The third pitfall to avoid is letting a venture studio be your primary or sole investor. Most venture studios come in on general terms, as they do not have enough capital for leading a round of investments. If you don't have other investors, your startup becomes too reliant on capital from the venture studio. That puts more pressure on the relationship and also limits resources for your company's growth. At Aleph One, we require a full-scale investment round with other investors doling capital to any startup we partner with. This way there is financial health in the company's growth, opportunity for scaling, and oversight from outside parties.

I want to pose a challenge to you: If you already have a dev agency working for you, set up a call with their CEO right now and ask if they would like to come in as investors. You should hear, "YES!" If you don't, you're in trouble. They are either not profitable or do not believe in your product. In this case, it's time to consider switching to a different dev agency or find a venture studio.

Summary

We've covered a lot of ground in this chapter. You should now have a basic understanding of the primary responsibilities of a CTO and the various camps in the CTO landscape, where you can seek candidates. There are numerous trade-offs with each camp and the summary table below captures the key takeaways.

Camp	Pros	Cons
Friends	Trustworthy	May not have managerial/leadership experience
Engineers	Technically savvy Typically have managerial/leadership experience Can hire and fire them as needed	May get stuck in a "developer" mentality and forget to consider long-term strategy High opportunity cost if you spend time and money on the wrong candidate
Development Agencies	Predictability in terms of cost and timeline	Conflict of interest You don't control their resources
Venture Studios	Trust reintroduced via investment	Rare You don't control their resources

A Checklist for Your Ideal CTO Candidate

There is much to consider as you navigate the CTO landscape and vet potential candidates. Any prospective CTO should have:

- baseline technical expertise (ideally, knowledge of several coding languages)
- recent managerial/leadership experience
- a willingness to put in a lot of hours immediately, with the understanding that their responsibilities will change in a few years

- the ability to do more than developer/engineer work, even as they receive a developer/engineer salary to begin with
- the right attitude and demeanor (trustworthy, excited, and open to challenges)

If you're looking for a more simplified checklist, remember the HIT-3-OUT-OF-5 list. Any CTO candidate must hit three of five of the following traits:

1. Senior software engineering experience
2. Product architecture experience
3. Team leadership experience
4. Project management experience
5. Previous (successful) CTO experience

No matter which camp(s) you explore to find your company's CTO, there will always be a give-and-take. Friends and venture studios are great options, but they have the smallest likelihood of coming to fruition and you need to take measures to ensure the partnership is set up well. As for the other two options—engineers and development agencies—setting up those relationships can be tricky. CTO-capable engineers are usually expensive, and dev agencies introduce a mercenary-esque attitude toward the work as well as conflicts of interest.

Once you've settled on your best option for CTO, it's time to roll up your sleeves and begin building the product specifications and structuring your foundational tech team. Get ready—you're going to start phasing your MVP!

Chapter 5:
Building Your Product Specs and Your Team

Now that you understand the responsibilities of a CTO, and the different camps in which a CTO may be found, let's shift our focus to your product. The first step in making your product a reality is building your product specifications, or specs. Then, once you have your specs, you can validate them with your CTO and plan the construction of your MVP and the long-term technical strategy.

As a non-technical entrepreneur, it can be easy to talk about your product at an idea level, yet drilling down to the details is harder. When the product is in your head, it is perfect. But building the product is when flaws surface, and you may realize some of your expectations are out of reach. Although certain challenges will be unavoidable in the product-building stage, many can be avoided with properly organized specs.

Getting your specs together is crucial to the functionality of your product because it forces you to answer three central questions:

1. What is the main value of the product?
2. Who is the target user of the product?
3. What is the core functionality that will deliver value to the customer?

If you are serious about your product, then you have intimate knowledge of the gap in the market you are targeting. You've done competitor research and perhaps created a pitch deck for your product. You know what the end result needs to be for your target user to benefit from your product, and therefore buy your product. When you can answer these questions, you can build your specs.

Getting Your Specs Together

Building your specs is something you can do by yourself or with your CTO. Most important is your knowledge of the market and the problem you are solving. I recommend building your specs by yourself, and then having your CTO validate them and advise on what technology is needed to achieve your goals.

So, what are specs? Specs detail the intended functionality of your product, often including extensive descriptions of what the functionality looks like at different stages. Specs can be anything from an elaborate pitch deck to detailed bullet points. While there is no set definition for specs, developers ideally need to see a visual representation of your product's functionality. For this reason, I recommend building specs together with wireframes.

Wireframes are visual blueprints of a web page or app,

outlining the placement of buttons, menus, and images without delving into the actual design or aesthetics. Short text describes the actions each button or link performs for the user. In creating wireframes, you'll use your imagination to compose screenshots of your realized product. We'll discuss wireframes and interfaces in more detail later in the chapter.

Before you can build your wireframes, though, you need to describe your product in words. Whether your product is an app, platform, or website, explain what it looks like and what it does. If you have notes or a pitch deck, compile all of those details into a single bulleted list. Don't worry about organizing the list yet. Just get everything down on the page. (In anticipation of organizing your notes, I recommend creating this list in Excel or Google Sheets.)

For example, let's say you're building a real estate website to compete with Zillow. Your list might include the following:

1. Homepage with the focus on search field, identifying user's target market

2. Map-based search results page, featuring available homes

   - Column on the side of a screen with card-based results along the map

   - Cards contain basic information about property—image, price, address, bedrooms

3. Advanced search filters, such as:

   - Location

   - Price range

   - Property type (e.g., single-family home, condo, townhouse)

- Number of bedrooms and bathrooms

- Square footage

- Year built

- Lot size

- Days on market

- School district

- Walkability score

4. Detailed property pages with:

- High-quality images

- Property description

- List of amenities and features

- Property history and tax information

- Mortgage calculator

- Virtual tours and/or video walkthroughs

- Neighborhood and community information

- Comparable nearby listings

5. User registration and login for personalized features, such as:

- Saving favorite properties

- Receiving notifications for new listings matching user's preferences

- Scheduling property viewings

- Contacting real estate agents directly

6. Agent profiles with:

- Agent photo and contact information

- License information

- Client reviews and ratings

- List of active and past listings

7. Integration with social media platforms for easy sharing

of listings

8. Mobile app for on-the-go property searches (this could even be expanded as a separate spec)

9. Blog or resource center with articles and advice for buyers, sellers, and renters

10. Analytics dashboard for agents to track listing performance and user engagement

Administrator analytics are often overlooked in specs, but you should be making notes about product analytics at this stage. This is especially true for B2B products, which will need their own platform division and functionality. Your CTO can help you with all of this, but start thinking about it early.

When building your specs, think about all the functionalities different types of users may have within their own portals. What are the differences between an agent's portal and a buyer's portal? What about an independent seller? Is there a verification process? You don't need to know *how* the verification process will work, but you must note you want one.

The same goes for payments and data security. How much of the data you collect will contribute to your company's value? For example, some companies thrive on reselling data they collect from users. Are you that type of company?

Write down as much as you can, and don't be surprised when you end up with four or five pages, *at least*. This is great! It can be easy to think more features mean more complexity, but that's not necessarily true. More detail means more *specificity*. And the more your CTO, and developers, can see what you're thinking, the better.

Getting specs together is typically the fun part for entrepreneurs. This is the idea phase. The reality of costs and timelines haven't kicked in yet, so dream big here. Don't hold back—you'll pare back the ideas soon enough.

After listing all your specs, the next step is to prioritize them. If you've created your list in Excel, this will be easy. Label your list of specs as "Specs" and then add a column with the label "Priority." In our real estate website example, every line from the specs will go to the Spec column, including subtasks for pages. Then, the Priority column will list one of three options: Top, Medium, and Low. Once the priority column is created, assign each spec a priority. Top priority represents the specs essential to the functionality of your product. In other words, Top priority specs are a part of your MVP. Medium priority specs are the additional features you think will be useful additions for users. And Low priority specs...well, don't be too attached to the features in this category—they typically end up in the trash bin. It is difficult to predict how a product will function and deliver value after the first round of feedback from users, let alone several rounds.

Once you have listed your specs and prioritized them, your CTO can then validate your thinking or suggest changes based on what they think is a realistic technical strategy. Fair warning, don't be surprised when they say, "Nope, that's low priority, this is low priority, and this—this is just crazy. Toss it out."

This is the point in the process where, for the first time, your CTO brings real value to your product. Here, they will begin to define a technical strategy for the product, considering available resources, timing, tech stack, team architecture, business priorities, and more. The technical strategy is coming into focus, and a product development plan begins to solidify.

The result of this spec-defining stage is a plausible, one-page description of an MVP. You might not like it, but this is an important part of phasing to build your product as quickly and cost-effectively as possible. If wireframes have not been part of the conversation yet, it is time to draft them.

Wireframes and User Interface Design

While the specs detail your product's functionality, wireframes and user interface (UI) design determine the actual user experience (UX). The first question the wireframes will answer is: How important is the user interface? If your product is B2B, in Fintech, B2D (business to developers), then the user interface may not be so important for the MVP and you can go straight to developing. But, in most cases, you'll focus on UI design as soon as you have wireframes.

A UI/UX designer is responsible for helping you design the frontend of your product, i.e. the user interface. They will help you build actual designs from your wireframes before you even start development. In other words, they are a pre-tech team.

To be clear, a UI/UX designer is not a graphic designer. A graphic designer creates visuals—logos, brochures, banners, etc. A UI/UX designer creates interfaces—website pages and app pages. UI/UX designers consider the user's intended purpose for interacting with the product and tailor the look and feel of the interface to encourage continued engagement and ease of use.

You'll typically hire a UI/UX designer early in the process because your developers will ask, "How do you want this to look?" But, if all you need is a functional interface to serve a specific purpose, then don't waste your time on design early on. You may devote resources toward building the MVP and working out bugs, and then hire a UI/UX designer later to polish it.

When you hire a UI/UX designer depends on how important the interface is to your product. This would be a discussion you want to have with your CTO, as well. They can suggest good generic designs from existing UI frameworks, templates, or even some AI-generated frontend designs.

Phasing to Your MVP

Whether you focus on design and then development, or go straight to development, your CTO must now think about the phasing of your product toward the MVP. You've described *what* your product is and does, and now you are thinking about *how* your product is going to be made. Phasing consists of three steps: estimating functionality, setting a timeline, and finally structuring a team.

1. Estimating Functionality

Functionality is usually estimated by a CTO. In this initial step, your CTO will determine how the various features of your MVP will interact. What infrastructure must be in place before certain features can be developed? How long will it take to build each feature? Who is responsible for developing each feature? Based on the complexity of the functionality and the number of different skills needed to develop the features, your CTO will begin planning a timeline, an estimated number of hours/days spent on each feature.

2. Set a Timeline

Your CTO will set a timeline based on your business and tech strategy. They will have to consider:

- What budget do we have?
- How many features (specs from the Top priority list) are required to be built for the MVP?
- Based on available talent, how many hours might it take to build the required features?
- How can we reduce the risks of not meeting estimates and expectations?
- How does the proposed timeline affect our go-to-market strategy as a business?
- Given available resources, which specs can we prioritize differently for the MVP stage to get to market quicker?

As a general rule, you want to phase to your MVP as quickly as possible. Therefore, you need to work closely with your CTO to set the timeline. Use your market expertise to help your CTO strategize phasing. However, keep in mind you cannot know how the market is going to react to your product. For this reason, the sooner you go to market with your MVP, the better.

Phasing to your MVP, and then to your full product, is all about iteration. If you wait too long, any number of things can happen—competitors may beat you to the market, the market may evolve so that your product is redundant, or you might simply run out of money. The ideal timeline from zero to market is two to three months. If your product is more complicated, four to five months might be reasonable. But an MVP that takes longer than six months signals you're wasting time. Only if your product is in the Wild category, with crazy new technology, could you consider taking six months or longer to build an MVP.

3. Structure a Team

With the specs listed and prioritized, the UI/UX design (possibly) underway, and a roadmap for your MVP set, you're ready to build the remainder of your team. Your CTO will have mapped out which roles are needed most urgently, and which roles can be phased in later. Some companies will need to hire a full in-house team from day one. This is usually only the case when the product involves sensitive business processes or sensitive data that cannot be shared with third parties—meaning, your business would be at risk if anyone outside the company had access to your business processes and data. However, this is the most expensive option and is to be avoided when possible.

Can You Afford to Hire a Team?

If you need an in-house team but don't have the funds, then this is a great time to start raising the funds! By this time, you have a CTO (or an agency), your specs, road-mapped phasing, and estimates for the cost to build your MVP and take it to market. But don't go straight to investors yet. Start by crowdfunding and/or having discussions within your network.

You can expect the cost to build your MVP and go-to-market to be around $50,000 to $120,000. This is a reasonable price for two to six months of work. This money covers developers, UI/UX (if not yet done), and marketers. Only approach institutional investors when you have an MVP, waitlist, or proven market interest in your product. Otherwise, you are likely to waste your time. A family-and-friends round for an MVP buildout is a reasonable way to raise giving out equity to people you know personally.

Once you have the funds to build the team, your CTO can start hiring people. To be clear, you don't need to make decisions when it comes to building the team. In fact, there's no clearer sign of a startup on the way to failure than a non-tech entrepreneur insisting on hiring a team of developers because they're cheap and fast. When those hires mess up, as a non-technical founder you will not know how to solve the problems. Let your CTO build your team.

Further, your CTO better understands the nuance involved with hiring different levels of engineers. You can't hire three senior engineers to work on a simple interface because they will be bored to death. You need a balance of junior, middle, and lead engineers. The junior engineers may focus on simpler tasks while the mid- to senior-level engineers work on more involved functionality tasks. Leave it to your CTO to gauge the level and number of engineers needed to build the product—they can balance the tech team as necessary.

While you don't need to make hiring decisions, you also don't want to be completely oblivious to how your team is being built. You may need to weigh in on which roles get filled first based on budget, for example. Your CTO might want to hire everyone right away, but some roles may not need to be filled until a few weeks or months into the process. Non-technical founders can benefit from a basic understanding of the key players on a tech team. So, let's take a closer look at the various roles on a tech team, and some of the technology they use.

Your Foundational Tech Team: Engineers and Related Roles

There are many possible roles on a tech team, and these roles can generally be broken into four categories: infrastructure (DevOps engineers), project managers/product owners, software developers and engineers, and quality assurance (QA) engineers. These are the basic roles to fill for any project. When you have the basic roles filled, then the team can grow and evolve.

Now, some of these functions could be taken on by founders and CTOs. Founders without technical background can do most of the pre-MVP quality assurance (QA) testing and product ownership duties. CTOs could take on any of these roles, based on their background. They can write software, take care of infrastructure, test the product, lead teams, and manage projects.

The remainder of this chapter will focus on the various roles of developers and engineers, and the related technologies your CTO will source as they work to build the MVP. In the next chapter, we'll explore how your team can grow with DevOps, project management, and QA.

Developers

There are many types of developers. The first type of developer we'll discuss is a web developer. Web developers are the people responsible for the functionality of your website. This involves work on both the frontend and the backend.

Web Developers

Frontend web developers are responsible for the functionality of the visible user interfaces. If a user clicks on a button that says "Subscribe," they are probably expecting a pop-up window to input their email address. Frontend developers convert these UI/UX elements into actual code so that the visuals function the way they're supposed to on the website.

However, the functionality on the frontend is not possible without the backend.

Backend web developers take care of databases and the accessibility of databases from the frontend, and they work on business logic. This is all the behind-the-scenes work of the website, the invisible functionality that makes a personality test spit out an answer, or a keyword search produce results. Backend developers take the business requirements, based on the UI design and specs, and create data structures and ways to manage those data structures.

While it is currently normal to split web developers into frontend and backend roles, this is unlikely to be done in the future. The all-inclusive role of a *full-stack developer*—who takes care of both the frontend and the backend—is becoming more common. Full-stack developers are most efficient when it comes to cost and timely delivery. They also tend to have more expertise. Full-stack developers have to know databases, data structures, server-side coding, business logic coding, and much more complex engineering than simply coding elements. They also know the visual elements must be scalable so that frontend components can be repeated or reused down the road.

Cross-platform Developers

If your product is a mobile or desktop app, you will want to consider whether it needs to be cross-platform or native. The difference between cross-platform and native platforms is that cross-platform architecture does not need code unique to each platform. Slack, Asana, Discord, Spotify, and Notion all started as cross-platform architectures, and some of them still are. The most common unification of code is between web and desktop, and also mobile, Android or iOS. So, for cross-platform products you would want to hire a full-stack web developer since most cross-platform code is written in JavaScript.

Native Mobile and Desktop Developers

When you're ready to scale your product, or it is platform specific, you'll need to hire native mobile and desktop developers. Native development differs from cross-platform development because it involves interaction with hardware (e.g., Bluetooth, drive storage, graphics, custom animations). Desktop games are usually native apps, but other products can be native, too. Clean My Mac is a great example of a native desktop app that efficiently searches a computer for useless or harmful code and clears it from the hard drive. This type of development requires knowledge of different coding languages, typically, C++, Java, native iOS, and Android interfaces. Therefore, you will need developers who specialize in various coding languages.

The approach to developing cross-platform or native mobile apps is similar. If your product doesn't need to access a device's storage (e.g., Bluetooth, GPS, recording devices, or camera), then cross-platform is a sensible way to scale. For example, think of most mobile library catalog apps. They're usually a cross-platform link to the library's web page with all the same features and functionality, just a slightly tweaked UI. That being said, they are usually slow.

If you want your mobile app to be more performant, then you usually want to develop a native app. In this case, all the screens are customized and animated to work with the native hardware and modules on the mobile device. This includes integrations with other devices such as watches, tablets, or monitors. These integrations aren't impossible with cross-platform development, but the performance is…not great. For example, Pokémon Go exploded in popularity because of its impressive integration with mobile modules—haptics, movement, vibrations, camera, augmented reality (AR), and so on. The game uses every aspect of mobile devices to immerse users in the game.

The Role of System Developers

In rare instances, a product will focus only on backend logic. Functionality is all that matters, and the interface is nothing more than a passing thought. For these products, you'll usually want to hire system developers.

System developers specialize in writing a few hundred lines of code (typically in C++ or Java) that can perform a task as efficiently as possible. A good example of this type of product is Citadel, a high-frequency trading platform. Citadel makes millions of dollars every day by making nanosecond-speed trades. The point of the product is to deliver high performance, via a server running independently with little human supervision.

Other Engineers for Your Product

Other categories of engineers are less common. The first is hardware engineers. Hardware engineers do embedded engineering, which means they write low-level code that works on microcontrollers in physical products. These are the people designing the chips that connect to the hardware in smart fridges, vending machines, ATMs, etc. (Not computers! Those are different.)

The other categories of engineers that you are unlikely to work with at an early stage are data engineers, AI engineers, and machine learning engineers. These are the analytical engineers who apply data science to your product. They usually work with Python and/or R. While you might work with these engineers at some point when building a Wild product, you probably don't need their input for your MVP. You can usually find these types of engineers hanging out on the AI community website, Hugging Face. This site hosts hundreds of thousands open source machine learning models on computer vision, natural language processing, audio processing. We will explore this later in chapter 9 about Artificial Intelligence.

Depending on your product and the advice of your CTO, you may only need to hire a few people to help get your MVP to market. Then, once the MVP hits the market and your business grows, you can start building the rest of your tech team, including DevOps engineers, project manager/product owner, and QA testers.

Chapter 6:
Growing Your Team
& Hiring an Agency

You have created your product specs and roadmap, and hired the first few developers to help you along the way. During this time, your CTO will be wearing a lot of hats. They may write code or act as a product owner. They may design and strategize. Or they might perform architectural, team leader, or project management duties. But as your team moves faster toward launching your MVP, your CTO will need to outsource most of these responsibilities to other team members. Therefore, it's important for you to understand the roles that fulfill these extra responsibilities.

A lot of confusion can arise when you don't know the difference between various roles on your team—specifically, the difference between the roles of product owner, project manager, DevOps engineer, and quality assurance (QA) tester. If you aren't familiar with these roles, you will likely think, "Wait, I thought I was the product owner and my CTO was the project manager. And the job descriptions of DevOps engineer and QA tester sound awfully similar to those of the project manager and product owner. What's the deal??"

At first, you are typically the product owner and your CTO is the product manager. But as your business scales, the responsibilities of these roles can be delegated to other full-time team members.

Further, if CTO responsibilities are being fulfilled by an agency instead of an individual, then you may think that the agency will take care of task delegation for you. But there are some caveats to this. There might be lag time if the agency is small and without sufficient resources to scale your product. And while you will still function as a product owner early on, having an agency function as your CTO means you may need to continually oversee and check the agency's outputs.

Setting up your tech team to scale with your product is a tricky process. By analyzing the various team roles and understanding how they execute your roadmap, you can effectively play your role as a founder and product owner. Whether your team is in-house or part of an agency, there are steps you can take to set everyone up for success. We'll cover these steps in this chapter. First, let's differentiate the common roles on a tech team.

Project Managers and Product Owners

Project managers (PMs) and project owners (POs) work closely together to deliver a product. When the product is your MVP, you can usually function as the PO, and your CTO can function as PM. After delivering your MVP and scaling your product, though, you will want to delegate these responsibilities to other full-time team members. So, what do these two roles do?

PMs are responsible for the engineering team's execution of daily tasks. They translate business requirements and roadmaps into short-term, iterative deliverables—also known as *sprints.* They also define bigger tasks as long-term goals, called *epics.* They often work closely with the PO to differentiate sprints from epics.

POs are charged with the functionality of the product. When the engineering team delivers on a sprint or epic, it's the PO's job to incorporate feedback from customers and prioritize new features as they align with overall business strategy. The PM then turns this feedback into daily and weekly tasks for the engineers to execute.

A common misconception is that the PO needs a certain level of technical expertise to make these decisions. For this reason, non-technical entrepreneurs will often try to teach themselves a little bit about code and technical infrastructure. While this usually doesn't hurt their ability to strategize about their business, it can tamper with decision making.

It might sound counterintuitive, but you *want* the PO to be a non-technical person. If the person in charge of functionality is technical, then the product will end up focusing more on technology and less on market fit. Keep in mind that technical people are not your average consumers. If the person in charge of functionality is also in charge of technology, you risk building a product that is incredibly efficient but incredibly bland.

At the MVP stage, you will usually be the PO and your CTO will be the PM, however, if your CTO doesn't have managerial expertise, you may want to hire a dedicated PM. A professional PM will help facilitate task management between your CTO and your developers and engineers. It's possible your CTO could receive training or mentoring from the PM so they can take on the responsibility.

In the best-case scenario though, your CTO has managerial experience and is skilled at breaking down specs and roadmaps into practical, short-term tasks with detailed descriptions. When you have a CTO with managerial expertise, you have more flexibility in what talent to hire for your team. You won't need to hire top-dollar developers and engineers to execute your product because your CTO will have defined small tasks that lower-level developers and engineers can execute. Your CTO will also be able to contract out work at an affordable rate and on an as-needed basis. This is the ideal setup for scalability, since you won't have full-time developers and engineers sitting on deck twiddling their thumbs and waiting for something to do.

While certain roles are easy to contract out, the addition of DevOps and Quality Assurance (QA) testing engineers tends to accelerate the daily progress of your tech team.

Development and Operations (DevOps) Engineers

The primary responsibility of a DevOps engineer is to design infrastructure that can deploy, secure, automate, scale, and monitor the product throughout its lifecycle. DevOps engineers are a crucial part of your tech team because they are responsible for the upkeep, security, and stability of mission-critical infrastructure. Think of them as the beating heart of your product. If there is an emergency, they are your first line of defense. They will wake up in the middle of the night and fix the issue. And if there is a requirement for the tech team to be delivering faster, the DevOps engineer will work with the infrastructure to speed up the pipeline. However, in the early stages, startups usually don't need full-time DevOps engineers.

In the beginning, most DevOps responsibilities can be handled by a CTO or your CTO can offload the responsibilities to a service (such as cloud automation-as-a-service, or application deployment-as-a-service). There are many ways to build faster, automated infrastructure early on without a DevOps engineer, which we'll discuss in the next chapter on scaling infrastructure.

In terms of roles and responsibilities, DevOps engineers are often confused with system administrators. A system admin is someone who makes sure all company hardware (computers) is working properly. They can do some basic automation, but they usually cannot write code—a trait that distinguishes them from DevOps engineers. In my opinion, you don't need system admins. If everyone in your company is working on Mac or Windows computers, and not downloading any "cracked" and unlicensed software, then you will never have the problems a system admin would be charged with fixing.

DevOps engineers are also often confused with server administrators. Server admins are the professionals who manage servers—nowadays, this often means cloud servers. The main difference between DevOps engineers and server admins is that server admins (like system admins) cannot write code and are not responsible for the full application development lifecycle and automation. Server admin expertise is limited to administering servers, security, and monitoring. DevOps engineering skills often include that of server admins as well as automation and management of the full development lifecycle.

Quality Assurance (QA) Testing Engineers

A solid tech team includes quality assurance (QA) testing engineers to avoid snafus with buggy code. Imagine attending a meeting with your investors, who are testing your product for the first time. The moment they start interacting with it, components break. All too often, this is because of buggy code.

Engineers are human, and when they work on hundreds of lines of code each day, they make small mistakes—hence the prevalence of buggy code. And after writing all that code, few engineers want to review it and look for their mistakes. So, companies hire people to test their engineers' code and document any inconsistencies with requirements. Ideally, these testers sign off on a project before it is released into production.

In the software engineering industry, there are two general types of testing: manual testing and automated testing. While it can be fun to test crucial functionality at the beginning of a project before the MVP launch, most QA engineers find ongoing manual testing tedious. Every time the product is updated with new features or new code, all pre-existing functionality must be tested, *in addition* to any new functionality before the updated product is released. QA engineers usually do this with a step-by-step guide following user stories (created earlier as a part of documenting functionality). While the process may only take 10-15 minutes to perform, it must be performed *every time the product is changed.* It can become mind-numbing work. (With advanced automation software, it is now typical to automate manual testing with software.)

Automation QA engineers write code to test existing functionality. This code, like other automation software, can turn the 10- to 15-minute manual process into a seconds-long process. QA engineers may tweak the testing code every so often, but for the most part this frees up another engineer's time from having to test everything manually.

You now have a better understanding of which roles typically make up a core tech team as a product moves toward MVP, and beyond. To bring those roles into your organization and scale your team, you have two options: Work with your CTO to recruit them directly, or work with an agency who can provide the necessary talent.

Working with an Agency

Working with an agency is another way to build your tech team, and it comes with pros and cons. If you've gone the agency route to build a Custom product, you likely have skipped hiring a CTO altogether. Fortunately, you can still scale your team working with an agency, and it's a common route for non-technical founders to take. The biggest drawback with an agency is that they have a conflict of interest, as their clients are embedded in their business model. Let's discuss how to screen agencies and explore what the process looks like when working with them.

For starters, an agency will likely assign you a PM who will take care of project management from the beginning. Further, an agency will save you from having to hire a team, retain them, do taxes for them, and other operational overhead. Along with PM, the agency will have existing processes to build, operate, and scale technical teams. You will be at the mercy of their technological excellence, which is why it is important to do your own research first.

Researching Agencies

When researching potential agencies to partner with, there are three steps you will want to take:

1. First, look at their expertise in the area of your product.
2. Second, look at their track record of previous projects.
3. Finally, get references.

These three steps make up your first filter when deciding

which agency to partner with, so let's break them down a little further.

The first step is to research the agency's domain expertise. In other words, does this agency have experience in the market your product is targeting? For example, if your product is related to Fintech, then your tech agency better have experience in Fintech. If they have never done a Fintech product before, then that's usually not a good sign.

When you partner with an agency, you are relying on them to have knowledge of your industry's technology. They must be aware of the recent industry innovations, existing tech they can apply to your product, and any certifications or legal requirements that must be met. In the case of Fintech, an experienced agency will have already been audited for security by a big four accounting firm (Deloitte, Ernst & Young (EY), PricewaterhouseCoopers (PwC), or Klynveld Peat Marwick Goerdeler) and they will know a range of data providers, tools, payment gateways, and regulations that must be followed to get your product to production. Stay away from inexperienced agencies endeavoring to get their hands on their first project in your industry.

Even if the agency *can* pull it off, there will be a learning curve that will slow down your two- to three-month path to delivering your MVP. You cannot afford to waste that time. Find an agency with prior industry experience.

Once you have collected a list of agencies with relevant industry experience, look at their track records. Which companies have they worked for? How long ago did they work for those companies? Which projects did they work on for those companies? And what is the current status of those projects and companies?

To set your expectations, don't be surprised if fifty percent of the sites on an agency's portfolio are in the web archives or Google cache. Lots of agencies build sites that never go anywhere. However, if *all* of the agency's projects are old, not functioning, or dead, you likely don't want that agency to deliver your product.

Try to identify each agency's successes. Look for projects that are for legitimate businesses and make money. These two factors are crucial because they indicate the agency managed to not only put a product through production, but also maintained the product and contributed to its success at some level. The more successes like this you find, and the more recent the successes are, the better.

The final step of research before hiring an agency is to speak with references. Get in touch with the companies who have worked with the agencies you are weighing. Ask each company if they would recommend the tech agency they worked with. Furthermore, you can ask each company what they liked and disliked about the agency they worked with. You're not asking for any confidential information, just a measure of how well it went and if the company maintains a positive working relationship with the agency.

Request Quotes

When you have a shortlist of prospective tech agencies to partner with, the next step is to request a quote from each one. A quote offers you insight into how the agency is structured and whether they are a good long-term fit.

In requesting a quote from an agency, you provide your product specs. Your specs will give the agency a sense of the scope of the project. For example, if you communicate that your target turnaround for the MVP is 2-3 months, the agency can determine how many people they would assign to the project and come up with a quote. The agency needs this information to give you an accurate quote.

Let's look at how you can engage with agencies and examine their quotes before making a decision.

Red Flags and Common Misconceptions

A realistic price tag for a Custom product is hard to estimate, but I would be vary of anything less than $15,000 per month (or $180,000 a year). Can web platforms be built for less? Of course they can! But when entrepreneurs underpay agencies for their products, they almost always end up losing more money in the long run. This is because cut rates are one of several red flags of agencies you want to avoid. Let's take a look at all the red flags.

Cut Rates

The first red flag you want to pay attention to is the use of cut rates. A lower-than-average rate from an agency is going to be appealing, but it's also a sign of bad business. If a business is too cheap, they are either not making money and/or underpaying employees. Sadly, it's not uncommon for an agency to underpay employees as a competitive advantage. But this is nonsensical because when employees are not paid well, they tend to leave.

A tech agency with high turnover is not sustainable. High turnover equates to higher costs of onboarding, changing developers, and transitioning roles. Further, the employees most likely to leave the agency are the most talented. So, even if the agency manages to stay staffed, it's unlikely they are retaining their talent long enough to maintain projects long after delivery.

This brings us to our first misconception about cut rates: many non-technical entrepreneurs think they can excuse a cheap up-front cost because they just need an MVP as soon as possible. "We can bring on better developers at a fairer rate down the road to grow the product, right?" Wrong. Don't fall into this trap. Agencies do not typically build your product, ship it to you, and send you on your way. Often working with an agency is closer to a partnership. Plus, it's difficult to move from agency to agency because the next people to get their hands on your product will likely have to start from scratch.

You want a team that is capable of not only building your product, but also scaling it. If they succeed, you succeed. And if you succeed, they succeed. But if the agency developing your product is at risk because their business is suffering, then that means your product (and therefore your startup) is also at risk.

Another misconception about cut rates is that the rates are relative to geography. This is true to some extent—developers in the US will cost a lot more than developers in the Philippines—but not to the degree most non-tech entrepreneurs imagine. No matter where in the world a developer resides, if they have the appropriate skills they can demand a competitive market rate.

Non-tech founders might believe that a lower rate based on geography is still appropriate because of a language barrier, but this is another misconception. The reality is that all documentation for industry standard coding languages is in English. So, if an engineer can speak English well enough to execute on tasks, then there is no language barrier. They can demand a fair and competitive salary from anywhere in the world. They don't need to accept a lower rate because of their location.

A cut rate may be appealing, but stay away from it. At the end of the day, going cheap will cost you more money in the long run. Buy cheap, buy twice, as the saying goes.

Even a 10% discount can be a red flag, because sustaining a healthy cashflow as a tech agency is a challenge. If you are offered a 10% discount, the agency is probably looking at a 2-7% profit at best. This small of a margin is too risky for a business partner. When an agency's profit is less than 10%, they cannot be prepared for top-level employees to take PTO. They cannot adapt as quickly to changes in the market. And they cannot be prepared for *force majeure* events like natural disasters, political turmoil, or war—problems that normally do not affect a tech agency with a healthy GPM.

Non-tech founders sometimes believe they cannot hire an agency that is based in an unstable region of the world, but herein lies another misconception. Developers don't need a lot of infrastructure to do their job—just WiFi, a laptop, and electricity to power it all. Because of this, if a region does become too unstable for them to work, they can relocate more easily than most other professionals. If an agency needs to relocate their team to a new city, the cost is usually not very high. So, avoid disqualifying tech agencies based on their region.

Here's the bottom line on cut rates: You want your tech agency to quote the industry average. No discounts. Whatever you've calculated your industry average to be, be prepared to pay that amount. Then you can start looking for other red flags.

Flat Rates

In an ideal agency, you want to see a feasible burn rate and a willingness to partner long term. If an agency returns a quote that says, "We can build your website in two weeks for $10,000," that might sound attractive, but that's not what you want to hear. You don't want a flat rate because that will not be a feasible burn if the project takes longer than expected.

What you want to hear is something like, "We'd be happy to work with you at a rate of $20,000 per month and it will take us six months to complete the work, based on the specs you provided and this kind of team." This is a better starting point because it shows openness to working long term and aligns with the industry average for a feasible burn rate. If an agency offers a flat rate and/or a fixed timeline, that's a red flag.

Exotic or Non-Industry Standard Tech

Another red flag you'll want to watch for when vetting tech agencies is the type of technology they use. You want your agency to use industry standard coding languages (such as the ones covered in the previous chapter). If an agency tries to sell you on any exotic tech you aren't asking for, back away.

I recently spoke with a startup based in Puerto Rico. They have a great founder and an interesting product in the insurance space, but they're partnered with an agency who uses a proprietary coding language—they call it their "no-code solution." When I pointed out to the founder his company is paying two full-time developers to customize the "no-code solution," he went wide-eyed. Unfortunately, the company is too far along with this agency to back out—they've spent six figures and six years building the tech. Yet, they're now struggling to scale and, to make matters worse, the IP isn't the founder's to sell—it belongs to the agency.

For most founders with Custom tech businesses, non-industry standard tech is a hindrance. Please be careful.

Agency Size and Ability to Scale

Okay, back to baseline. Another red flag to beware of when vetting tech agencies is size. Keep in mind, when an agency is acting as your CTO, *they will need to scale with your product.* This means hiring additional talent as needed. If the agency is too small (say, under 15 people), such that they don't have the capacity to hire and integrate new talent quickly, they may be unable to scale with your product. Therefore, they are not the best fit.

Boutique tech agencies of less than about 30 people are usually good options, if they have expertise in your area. This is a good size for an agency to serve multiple clients in a specialized area of technology and still have some flexibility to transition and expand as needed. Their overhead costs are not as high as other larger companies because they are still a small company.

A bigger agency can also be a good fit, but they tend to require a bit higher burn rate to start with. They have much higher overhead costs simply because of their size. However, size can often be a sign of a stable and healthy business. So, if a bigger agency is quoting slightly above the industry average, don't count them out if you can afford it.

Large Time Difference

The last factor you want to consider when vetting an agency is their time zone. Time difference is a big factor when establishing regular communication with your tech partner. Any time difference up to six or seven hours is acceptable, as you can still connect during regular working hours. A nine-hour time difference is still feasible, but less ideal as one side will have to stretch their workday a bit to accommodate. A 12-hour time difference is terrible. Forget it. It's not going to work if you can only connect with each other as you are waking up or going to sleep. That kind of communication is too slow to be sustainable.

A Green Flag

Consider asking the tech agency to invest in your product. They may not go for it, but your willingness to partner with them will often be well-received and will establish a foundation of trust. Who knows, they may really believe in your product and invest five to six figures! There is no harm in asking—you'll want all the financial support you can get. Running Aleph One for over seven years now, I can say we only work with companies we can invest in. This puts us on the same side of the table, eliminates conflict of interest, and eases the financial burden for entrepreneurs.

Ready, Set, Grow

Whether your CTO is an individual or tech agency, you want to take time early on to properly set up the partnership. The road to your MVP might be short, but growing and scaling your product is a long and windy path. At first, you will be able to function as the PO, coordinating with your CTO who will function as the PM (whether that's your CTO or the PM assigned to you by your tech agency). Between the start of your journey and the delivery of your MVP, you may only need the help of one or two additional developers. After your MVP hits the market, though, you need to make sure your team scales with your product. You need to make sure your tech team is well structured to communicate and execute tasks as efficiently as possible.

With an internal team, the bigger your team grows, the faster your burn rate will be. Certain members on your team— namely QA and DevOps engineers—will play their part to try and improve efficiency, but as your product grows in complexity and market feedback comes in, task management will become more time consuming. And you don't want your CTO spending all their time assigning tasks. As you scale, look to hire a PM as fast as you can so your CTO has more time to work on optimising processes and higher level engineering.

Similarly, as you scale, you don't want all of *your* time to be owning the functionality of the product. With market feedback coming in, hire a dedicated PO to organize feedback on functionality and work with the PM to strategize sprints and epics. This will give you the time you need to keep marketing your product to investors and new customers.

Scaling successfully requires a delicate balance between burn rate and what you can actually afford with available investment and revenue. You usually only get one shot at striking this balance, but you can do it. After all, the best is yet to come. You still need to develop your product from MVP to fulfillment of your initial idea. To do this, you'll need to develop a faster, automated infrastructure that can scale with your product.

Chapter 7:
Setting Up and Scaling Technical Infrastructure

OK, you've got an idea of the kinds of people who will be joining your technical team, and a timeline for when they'll be joining, but what about the technology itself? It's time to talk about your product's technical infrastructure—what it is, how it is set up and by whom, how to stabilize it, and how to scale it.

Regardless of whether you're building a simple, custom, or wild product, your technical infrastructure consists of a lot of moving pieces. It consists of the physical or cloud-based servers that provide access to your product and the codebase for product. It incorporates all the automated systems that stabilize and scale your product. And it involves engineers and developers who fix problems and work on new developments. Generally speaking, your technical infrastructure is all the technology working together to ensure consumers have a seamless interaction with your product at all stages of its growth.

To build, stabilize, and scale your infrastructure in a way

that keeps your product competitive, your CTO and their tech team must be ready to move fast. You cannot wait for developers to get back from holiday to fix bugs. If your site crashes, the right people need to be notified immediately so they can start fixing the problem *immediately*. Technical infrastructure problems are common, usually urgent, and they often fall outside the standard nine-to-five workday. The work of maintaining this infrastructure is a marathon, but you and your team can do it.

Going from your MVP to production, and from production to scaling, entails different styles and approaches to technical infrastructure. Each phase will involve cloning and backing up your codebase, preparing new servers for different roles in the company to work on the product, and automating as much as possible so your infrastructure can grow exponentially. It's a high-stakes balancing act—one that your CTO must help your company perform with precision.

So, let's discuss your technical infrastructure in the context of the four general phases of product development—MVP, production, stabilization, and scaling—and explore your CTO's responsibilities during each phase. We'll start with the MVP phase, when your infrastructure is generally fluid. Here, developers have the freedom to experiment hands-on with every area of the product with minimal consequences. Next, we'll look at how your infrastructure will change when you move to production, and mission-critical environments become a necessity. Then, we'll explore what must happen to your infrastructure when the primary focus becomes product stabilization. And finally, when stabilization is achieved, we'll look at the phase you're probably already dreaming about: scaling your product and infrastructure. Ready? Let's go!

Get Started with MVP Infrastructure

When you're building your MVP, you don't need a solid infrastructure. This is because you don't yet have customers interacting with your product. You don't need to worry about Sally from North Carolina logging into her account because her account doesn't exist yet. The only people interacting with your product are the people working on it. This means you can be a bit loose with your infrastructure during this time.

In Facebook's early years, the company famously embraced the mantra "Move fast and break things." And, during the early days of your startup, you can feel free to do the same. Your product isn't going to production yet, so you don't need to have a stable, production-ready environment. You don't need to have mission-critical systems that are monitored 24/7. You don't even need to back up your database yet because it hasn't been populated with actual information. You haven't launched the website, launched on the app store, or gone to market in any other capacity. If the product suddenly breaks, so what? Your developers learn to fix it with no pressure beyond a 2- to 4-month MVP deadline.

While your developers have fun experimenting with your product, it's easy to become stressed. After all, this is *your* product. You don't want it to break, you want it to work. However, your product is going to break—it's only a matter of how and when. You might not be able to control the *how*, but you can influence the *when* by encouraging your tech team to be as experimental as possible during the MVP stage. Let developers break the product now, rather than users breaking it after launch. It will be better for your product, and it will increase morale for the next stage.

It is important to understand that during the early stages your tech team is tinkering with your product all the time. So, if you have an investor meeting before launch and you want to show off your product's progress, be sure to tell the tech team, "Hey, I'm meeting with potential investors tomorrow from 1-2pm Eastern Time. Please don't touch the product until after I talk to them." At any time before launch, your product may have flaws or down time as your tech team fiddles with the frontend and backend. This is acceptable leading up to the MVP launch, but after you launch, the product should be on a path toward becoming more stable.

Now, what about your CTO? What are they up to during this first phase? Right now, they are probably wearing a lot of different hats as they write and test code, collect feedback from you, and manage another developer or two to build the MVP. And that's in addition to their strategic responsibilities. They can still be working full-time, but they won't need to delegate too much work yet. That usually doesn't happen until you're ready to launch your MVP and move toward production.

Create Production-Ready Environments

Before your MVP goes to launch, you will need to build production-ready environments. While developers were hands-on 24/7 with your product during the MVP stage, they now need to know when they must be hands-off. This can start by your implementing *stable phases*—time periods when developers agree *not* to touch the product—but it will eventually need to evolve so your product has environments where it can live safe from any radical changes by developers.

When the product goes to production, it must have a level of stability. There is a clear transition that must happen before the infrastructure is ready for market. This transition involves a few changes, which we'll discuss now.

Upping the Infrastructure Budget

The first change that must happen before your product is production-ready is increasing the span of infrastructure costs. This might sound obvious, but most founders overlook this step. In addition to paying for salaries, tech licenses, and probable legal fees, you need to budget for additional servers for your product. And there are different types of servers you will need.

Backing Up to New Servers

It might not make sense to have a high level of redundancy during development, but when you go to production you need to back up your database continuously. Almost every production system today has some form of continuous backup because the consequences for losing data are astronomical. Imagine an ecommerce site receiving a few too many orders at one time, crashing, and then *losing the orders!* Just when business is about to be great, it's suddenly at its worst.

I know of one media company that unfortunately lost all of its data and didn't have a backup. They managed to salvage their site, but it was a messy process. They had to dig through Google Cache to find a cached version of their website, download that, and then restore all of their media files, descriptions, meta tags, and more. Not fun.

Some cloud-based servers offer this kind of continuous backup. Amazon and their RDS cloud database service is one. But this service requires you to split your development and production environments. This is common as the more infrastructure you have, the more stability is needed for your production environments. We'll revisit this problem in the next section.

Of course, you don't *want* your product to break, so the next step in preparing your infrastructure for MVP launch is to set up additional servers for the spike in post-launch traffic. These are not the same as backup servers but are *additional* servers that will help diffuse the demand on your product when you receive a spike in users. This problem can be hard to visualize, so let's consider a couple of analogies.

First, these types of servers play a role akin to old-fashioned call center operators. Call center operators received inbound telecommunications and patched callers through to their intended receivers. During low-traffic times, only one or two operators were needed on the job. But during high-traffic times, the call centers were packed to the brim with operators patching the thousands of callers.

Now, imagine pitching your product on the show *Shark Tank* and getting a big offer from the investors. Then, the moment the episode airs you get thousands of viewers trying to engage with your product. How many servers will you need to "patch through" the inbound traffic to your product? In the same way that you cannot have thousands of people typing on a keyboard at once, you cannot have thousands of people engaging with your product on *one server*. You need the infrastructure to be ready to receive the traffic and provide consistent and dependable access to your product's functionality.

This scenario begs the question: What do you do with all of your servers when the spike in traffic subsides? We'll discuss this in the next section. For now, let's wrap up what you must do to prepare your product to launch in the first place.

Freezing Code

The last step in preparing your product for MVP launch is implementing a system of code freezes. While the code is changing practically every day during development, it must go through periods of time when it is static for production. These static periods are the code freezes. Once these are in place, your Project Manager can implement sprints and epics to update the code. These are called "development cycles."

You probably know that when any of your apps update from the app store, their version number will tick upward: 1.3.1, 1.3.2, 1.3.3, 1.4.1, and so on. While you engage with one version of the app on your device, developers are doing a sprint in a separate production environment to prepare the next iteration of the app. When you update the app, you get the new version with the developers' updates installed and no changes to your data. It appears so seamless from your side as the consumer, but on the other side there is a lot of infrastructure and processes in place to make sure the code gets updated without negatively affecting the data.

There are instances when developers will go in with their bare hands and work on the active product's code. These instances are usually when there are mission-critical issues such as bugs or breakages in the crucial components of the system. When these problems arise, users need a fix ASAP.

Your CTO's Role Pre-MVP Launch

Preparing infrastructure for the MVP launch is complicated and expensive, but this is why you have a top-tier CTO to navigate this crucial phase of your product's growth. While your CTO was probably writing a lot of code and having fun messing around with your product for a few months, they are now stepping into a managerial role. They may hire junior developers to maintain the code and handle the small problems that arise. They may work with engineers to prepare the number of servers your product needs to go to production.

Your CTO is rushing toward your MVP launch deadline, and as soon as your product launches, everyone's work will multiply. If infrastructure is in place to absorb the spike in usership, the work will be manageable. Your team can contain the chaos. This is where you and your CTO's work to stabilize the product begins.

Stabilize Your Product

After launching an MVP, most founders want to immediately start scaling. But scaling an unstable product only creates bigger problems down the road. So, before you scale your product, you must *stabilize* it.

Stabilizing your product involves working on several areas of your infrastructure. First, you need to evolve the iteration cycles so new code is tested and quality assured before pushed through to production. Second, you must engineer solutions to increased traffic and user fluctuations. And third, your DevOps engineer needs to automate as much of your architecture as possible. Let's walk through each of these areas in detail.

Integrate QA Testing into Delivery Flow

The first step in stabilizing your product is to adjust the iterative cycles of development and production. Before MVP launch, your CTO worked hard to establish different environments for developing, staging, backing up, and pushing to production.

But when users are interacting with your product 24/7, these four environments are insufficient.

Just because you have designated development and production environments doesn't ensure the launched product is safe from development errors. User experience is now a reality, so the stakes are higher. You must be 100% certain about new code before pushing it out to the production repository. This is where QA testing comes into play.

Not all systems have QA testing, but in my opinion testing is necessary. Remember, developers are human, and they will make mistakes. Plus, developers can lose sight of how their new code will interact with rapidly growing infrastructure. The earlier you can catch the mistakes, the better.

Not all QA testing is the same, so you will need pipelines in place that help developers and QA engineers push updates efficiently. For example, new functionality demands manual testing—literally by hand on a phone or laptop—to see how the whole product works with the new feature. (It's startling how often the addition of a new feature disrupts the functionality of other features.) And, developers working on mission-critical business logic—like a current version's functionality—will often need a routine process of QA testing at the end of every development cycle.

QA testing can take a copious amount of time, especially if it's not automated. But you cannot stabilize and scale your product if QA testing isn't integrated into your delivery flow. You don't want to update your website only to discover that users accessing it on an older version of Safari don't have all of the new functionality. Thankfully, there are ways to automate much of the QA testing systems, which we'll examine shortly.

Dealing with Fluctuating Traffic

The second step toward stabilizing your product is dealing with growing traffic and any volatile fluctuations in use. Your product might be bulletproof when only a handful of people are using it, but what happens when there are a hundred, ten thousand, or a million users at one time? In the previous section, we visualized this problem as a call center with not enough operators. But what happens when the call center is simply too small? Sometimes the problem isn't so much with the number of servers, but how the servers are designed.

For example, imagine that your MVP is monolithic—meaning, all of its functionality is executed on one server. Perhaps it is an app that takes images uploaded by users and resizes them to users' likings. An algorithm that executes this kind of functionality is complex and would demand 100% of the CPU's processing power. Not a problem when only one person is using the app—but what if ten people are on the app at the same time?

Consider the problem that will arise if the app is resizing one user's image while another user is trying to sign up and upload their own image. Normally, there are synchronous programming techniques where you can engineer tasks to be performed simultaneously by one CPU. But if the app is monolithic, then you still have only one CPU responsible for running *everything*—your APIs, sign-ins, sign-ups, uploads, and everything else. So, when a heavy-duty task like resizing an image occurs, everything else freezes while the complex task is executed.

Imagine ten users waiting to sign in because an app is busy resizing someone else's image. It's silly. Nobody wants to wait more than a few seconds to sign in. Thankfully, this kind of problem has a number of engineering solutions.

In this example, your CTO might suggest stabilizing the product by introducing scalable engineering techniques, such as microservice architecture. This means having different physical machines responsible for different functions of the app, but they all work in tandem. One or two servers can be dedicated to resizing images while other servers take care of authorization and other tasks. It's worth noting, though, that this is not only an adjustment to infrastructure, but to code design, too. Moving from monoliths to microservices is a major engineering project, but this might be the kind of stabilization and team organization upgrade you need before you can scale.

One common misconception among non-technical founders is that servers are part of the product. Meaning, once a server is added, it's hard to remove or replace it. This is not the case. Remember, think of servers like call center operators. They are not assigned to users in the sense that they are storing data on users. The data is in your product's database, which is usually stored on a cloud network—one that was either built by your tech team or (more realistically) sourced. The servers are the access points connecting users to the database, and the number of active servers can increase or decrease with the number of anticipated users. *How* the number of active servers increases or decreases is a part of DevOps engineering work.

Automate With the Help of DevOps

The third area of your infrastructure that must stabilize before your product can scale is its automation. The person in charge of automating your infrastructure is your DevOps engineer, and one of their first tasks is to automate your product's anticipated load capacity.

The *anticipated load capacity* is the number of people you expect to be requesting access to your product's database at any given time. The stability of your product relies on your infrastructure's ability to accurately anticipate the load capacity. It's one matter to have enough available servers to handle a spike in users, but it's an expensive problem to keep all of those servers when the spike subsides. So, not only do you need a way to scale down the number of active servers when they aren't needed, you need a way to scale them back *up* when another spike in users is expected.

It would be way too time-consuming for one person to manage the number of active servers, because it is a continuous process. After your MVP launches, people from around the world can access it at any time. And accurately predicting spikes in users is not a foolproof process. Thankfully, there are programs that can automatically track users in real time and scale up or down the number of active servers to accommodate. This is usually one of the first things your DevOps engineer will be responsible for managing.

Another responsibility crucial to infrastructure stability is establishing an automated system of alert protocols. Remember, when your product goes to production, *things will break.* This is to be expected, not avoided. So, part of preparing for this reality means setting up programs that check for errors and alert the right engineers to fix problems when they occur.

While your CTO might set up the initial alert protocols—such as a system that checks your website every five minutes to make sure users can still log in—they cannot create these systems for all the areas of the product that must be monitored. When your product is live, feedback loops quicken from users and your CTO will likely be handling mission-critical infrastructure problems. But the number of possible instabilities, errors, infrastructure hiccups, and functionality breaks is incalculable. You need a team that is focused on creating systems to monitor all of these things—this is typically your lead DevOps engineer and their team.

You can think of these alert protocols like Gotham Police spotters. Crime and chaos can break out anywhere in the city, at any time and in any form. The spotters must know when to notify an officer in a neighborhood, and when to light up the Bat Signal. The problem is that the spotting is manual, and so the time between a problem arising and Batman being notified is sometimes too long.

How do you get the superhero on the job faster? Make all of the spotters automated programs, apply all of the crime and chaos to your product, and know that every engineer in your company will have their own version of the Bat Signal. (Obviously, your CTO gets *the* Bat Signal.) Now, nobody needs to "watch out" for problems because automated systems are logging them and alerting your trusty superheroes in real time. This frees up hundreds of human work hours to focus on other areas of your product and its stabilization.

Quicken Transfer Speeds with CDNs

Finally, depending on the size of your market, your DevOps engineer may be responsible for setting up a Content Delivery Network, or Cloud Delivery Network (CDN). Let's say you are building an app that can resize images. Your algorithm is intuitive, efficient, and growing in popularity. People all over the world now want to download your app and resize their images. This sounds great, right? Well, yes, but beware a big problem.

If your server is based in New York and a user in Australia wants to upload an image, how does the image get from Australia to New York and back? For one byte of data to travel between NY and Australia it takes about 200 milliseconds on average. While this is not looking like much, if you add bigger data sizes, server processing time — it could add up to seconds. Several seconds in modern age is too much to ignore when scaling your product. For example, Google ranking algorithm penalises websites which load for longer than 2 seconds and don't have high availability across the world.

A DevOps engineer can speed up long-distance information transfer speeds by building (or more likely employing) a CDN. A CDN is basically a network of high availability servers that proactively clone data in various geographical locations. This shortens the distance that information must travel to reach the nearest server in a network. With a CDN in place, your app could be cloned on a server in Australia so that the transfer process only takes a few seconds instead of more than a minute.

Of course, cloning your product across a network of servers once doesn't solve anything. The moment the next version of your app launches, the process will need to repeat. This is another area where the DevOps engineer's work is key. It's one thing to work with a pre-established CDN (like Amazon CloudFront, for example), but it's another to build systems for automatically keeping the CDN up to date with the most current version of the product at all times. This is a complex system—you can expect your DevOps engineer to dedicate a lot of time to building it.

While your tech team works on stabilizing your product, your CTO will have their hands full. First, they will be busy managing new iterative systems for implementing formal QA into your pipeline. Then, they will rush to expand the physical architecture of your product so it can handle greater fluctuations in users. Finally, they will be collaborating with a DevOps engineer to automate technology throughout the company and prepare the product to scale. But they have still not reached the peak of their responsibilities. That comes in the next phase.

Scale Your Product with Good Leadership

You have a stable environment for your launched product. New features are routinely tested by QA engineers. Automated systems are tracking, logging, and alerting engineers to problems. Infrastructure is in place to manage load capacity in real time. And your production pipeline is flowing with exciting new developments. You have all the stability you could ever ask for and you are itching to finally scale your product.

You have good reason to be excited. If done right, this can be the most lucrative phase of your business growth—the moment you realize the potential value of your company, make a big splash in the market, and start waiting for the investment offers to flow in. While this can be an amazing time in your life as a non-technical founder, you must remain tightly connected to the tech side of your company. While your tech team might seem as self-sufficient as ever, now is the time that they need your leadership the most.

Scaling is a different game from stability because it creates as many human problems as it does technical ones. The first common human problem is that while the product grows, the company is also growing, yet important internal communication tends to slow down as teams and work become siloed. The second common problem is one of morale. As the work becomes more automated, tedious, and less creative, teams lose motivation to solve the problems that *do* arise. Finally, when you scale your product, your tech team and its leaders will have to address the most aggravating problem plaguing every tech company: technical debt. Let's discuss each of these problems, starting with internal communication.

Create Documentation to Streamline Internal Communication

The first problem that any company faces when it scales is streamlining communication between departments. As a company grows, communication channels get cluttered. Slack threads pile up with documents and code all over the place, and new additions to the team usually have a hard time getting up to speed. Feedback from clients and customers comes in at faster speeds and in greater quantities, while customers demand faster turnarounds. Product fixes and new developments need to be in production sooner. And the people responsible for addressing these matters can't wait for their supervisors, or their supervisors' supervisors, to be available to advise them in their work.

What you need is for every person to come on board knowing exactly what their responsibilities are and *how* to go about handling their responsibilities. When the team was small, your CTO and a handful of team leaders could instruct everyone on what to do. But, as you scale your product, your team will scale up, too. So, how do you ensure more people know how the platform actually works when the most experienced team members are less accessible? One word: documentation.

The key to establishing efficient interdepartmental communication with a growing team is creating documentation. Not only must engineers do their work, but they must document their work so a future engineer can replicate it. You can't have all your developers doing things slightly differently! You must have regularly updated internal documentation on how to use the platform and write code because, by default, your growth means engineers have more onboarding to do with new developers.

Your tech team will have onboarding protocols that can only be as effective as your documentation. This means written and replicated descriptions on infrastructure, development flow, tool functionality, how to write code, and how the architecture is structured. And all of this documentation will be unique for each type of engineer—frontend, backend, full stack, QA, DevOps, and so on. *And* as the tech team grows in scale, so must the documentation. It's ongoing work and it never ends, but thorough documentation is crucial to protecting your growing product from errors made by new developers and to ensure all team members are working most efficiently.

Build Team Morale

When your team grows, it becomes harder to retain and recruit developers. This is because as your project scales and gets massive, the codebase starts to look more like a legacy project. It's huge, and therefore it's more static. And it's hard for developers to have fun in a relatively static environment. It is possible, though, to maintain morale with the help of good leaders who can implement incentives, rewards, and even gamify the work to keep developers interested and engaged.

Developers prefer to work in more dynamic environments, like the one your startup had when it was in the early MVP development days. Those are the environments where developers can learn more, grow on a personal level, and have the most fun. After all, it's fun to "move fast and break things." But when you are scaling, the motto is more along the lines of "Don't screw anything up, *please*." There is still important work to do, but it can become less creative.

Quality leadership keeps the team excited and fit to take on new challenges. While the work may not be as fun, there are still complex problems to solve. You and your leaders must promote the exciting side of the company's tech to keep team morale high. (This can also help when recruiting new talent.) At this stage of your company's growth, your dev leaders not only understand how the tech works, they understand *people*.

Manage Technical Debt... Sooner Than Later

The third problem standing in the way of scaling your product is an ugly monster: technical debt. Technical debt is not financial debt. Rather, it is the sum of all the corners your tech team may have cut while optimizing for speed of delivery rather than quality. Dealing with technical debt is not fun—it's a bit like dealing with a stinky pile of dirty laundry.

Technical debt starts piling up from the early days of your company. When the priority is to release new developments as quickly as possible, developers tend to do something called "extreme programming," meaning they work fast and cut corners. While this is fine in the short term, it does compromise architecture, code quality, code stability, and ultimately code scalability. And if you don't pay attention to technical debt at the scaling stage, then a once-manageable pile of dirty laundry will become an impossible mountain of stink.

When put in perspective, dealing with technical debt sounds obvious, but in practice the task requires a lot of intentionality. After all, dealing with technical debt doesn't bring in any new revenue. This makes it easy to overlook when you want to prioritize new sales or new features. Those projects make more money in the short term. But the more your technical debt piles up, the greater the potential avalanche of problems down the road.

Accountable technical leadership will make sure technical debt is being accounted for at all times. Now that you're getting more users and scaling your product, it's time to deal with technical debt issues and setting up systems to address it on a regular basis.

Your CTO's
Scaling Responsibilities

You have a stable product. You have leadership that has over-seen the creation of documentation, boosted team morale, and addressed the sobering reality of technical debt. You finally have a product that can scale! But where does this leave your CTO? Well, their responsibilities have scaled, too.

At first, your CTO was your firefighter. They rolled up their sleeves and got their hands dirty fixing code, managing developers, testing their code, and building out your archi-tecture. Then, as they hired more team members, they took on more of a managerial leadership position. But then even those responsibilities got delegated to other senior leaders. So, what is your CTO doing now? Well, now they may be a fully realized Chief Technical Officer. They are fielding requests all day long from other department heads, tech managers, company clients, prospective clients, and you.

And guess what? When your product scales and grows, the number of requests your CTO has to deal with increases, too. One new category of people trying to grab time with your CTO will be your competitors.

When your product goes to scale and makes a splash in the market, competitors will take notice. You will get a nice bite of the market for a time. Savor it. It's only a matter of time before another company figures out what you're doing and fights for their own piece of the pie. And if your CTO isn't working closely with you to position your technology and your company to remain competitive, you will be pushed out. So, for your CTO, scaling is the ultimate phase in your company's technical strategy. And this phase is when they will really prove their worth.

Chapter 8:
Welcome to the Wild West

Chapter 7 took us through the general process of bringing your product from MVP to production to a scalable platform. This is a common trajectory for Custom products. However, even if you are sure your product falls into the Simple or Custom categories, you can benefit from an awareness of what companies with Wild products do differently and how they utilize new, sophisticated technology.

A company doesn't need to have a Wild product to integrate Wild technology. For example, a Simple ecommerce shop could make and sell NFTs. A Custom service provider could accept crypto payments. Anyone can integrate an AI-based chatbot to help with incoming customer requests and prioritize customer feedback.

Building a Wild product to make your company more defensible, more competitive, and more valuable is a whole different ball game. And that is the game we'll examine in the final part of this book. In this chapter, we'll cover how Wild products differ from Simple and Custom products, and how your approach to acquiring a CTO must be different when building a Wild product. Then, in the following chapters, we'll look at a few specific technologies used in Wild products, how startups building these Wild products must approach their industry differently, and how platforms for Simple and Custom products can benefit from the commoditized parts of these Wild products.

Integrating Technology Versus Inventing Technology

There are a few ways Wild products differ from Simple and Custom products, but the main difference is that Wild products involve **the invention of a new business model and/or the invention of new technology**. Any time there is innovation and patents at the heart of a business model, the product is almost certainly Wild. Simple and Custom products can integrate technology used in Wild products, but unless they are developing new technology or inventing a new business model around the technology, they are not Wild.

Platforms for Wild products are generally unprecedented, but there are a handful of categories we will zero in on for this book. Specifically, we will look at sophisticated technologies like AI, blockchain, machine learning, AR/VR, and the Metaverse—technologies that can generally be integrated by Simple and Custom product platforms without the help of a tech genius. We will not be looking at hardware companies in sectors like biotech, med-tech, and space flight.

Before you get too excited by the idea of inventing new Internet technology, though, let me offer a brief reality check based on my experience. Almost every week I have a conversation with a non-technical entrepreneur that goes something like this. After introductions and chit-chat, they say something along the lines of, "So, here's my idea for a new type of AI." Then they proceed, stone sober and dead serious, to explain to me how they think this hypothetical AI will be groundbreaking in their industry and open doors to a number of lucrative opportunities.

I have these conversations all the time, and the challenges are always the same. First, most entrepreneurs don't have the capacity to innovate AI technology. Many conflate cloning, integrating, or repurposing existing technology with creating new technology. Second, they don't have a technical partner.

While their ideas are exciting, these entrepreneurs are failing to recognize that when you pursue a Wild product you cannot follow paved roads. To put it plainly: the fact that they are talking to me—the head of a venture studio—means they are likely following conventional methods, and their product likely isn't Wild.

Let's back up a bit. Where, exactly, did these entrepreneurs go wrong?

To Build a Wild Product, You Need an Internal CTO

In all cases where a new business model with new technology is involved, you need a full-time, in-house CTO. And not just any CTO. You will need a CTO who has:

- an expertise and commitment to fulfilling the technical requirements of the role,
- the flexibility to keep the new business model agile, and
- a head for safeguarding company property (required for the company to be defensible).

These requirements ultimately rule out agencies as tech partners. Yet there are more reasons why agencies are a poor choice.

Agencies are not designed to spearhead innovation, but rather to follow innovation. You cannot hire an agency and say, "Please invent this new technology I have in my mind— don't worry, I'll explain it to you." Agencies are a business with systems and processes, and they can't accurately plan how to manage a project for an unknown product. Agencies can follow a paved path, but they cannot help other companies pave new paths.

Even if an agency has invested capital in a startup (a sure sign of commitment), they are not set up to succeed. Reliability is not the problem—the problem is that, with a Wild product, a CTO's responsibilities are all-consuming. The CTO will be writing code, architecting new infrastructure, troubleshooting, problem solving, innovating, and producing every day. It is a full-time job, if not more. Agencies work on several projects at once, but a Wild product requires a dedicated CTO.

Now, it's possible an agency has the resources to help an internal CTO, then the agency can assist with solving specific parts of a problem. But even then, this approach is suboptimal. The broken relationship between Tesla and NVIDIA makes this clear. Tesla's top objective is to develop self-driving cars, which is hands-down a Wild product. Part of developing this product involves the production of high-performance, energy efficient computer chips. They initially partnered with NVIDIA—one of the world's top computer chip developers—to produce these chips. However, when it came to testing the chips for their performance and energy efficiency, Tesla ran into problems.

Tesla is first and foremost a software company but, like all software, they require specific hardware to function optimally. In their case, the hardware they were working with was NVIDIA chips. Now, the software for Tesla's self-driving cars could not be tested in a traditional testing lab. Tesla needed to build a special testing lab uniquely equipped to evaluate the technology for their cars. This meant that Tesla needed to know everything about how the chips were designed and developed in order to build the lab and perform the tests. And this was information that NVIDIA was not eager to provide.

As long as Tesla was assuming full responsibility for their technology, they required full control over the development of their product. They needed to control every step of the process, and they didn't have time to negotiate with NVIDIA. So, Tesla ditched their partnership.

In NVIDIA's place, Tesla hired a top-of-the-line engineer who was an expert in neural net hardware. They tasked this engineer with designing a lab to test and then further develop the chips. This put Tesla in full control of the development of their product, both the software and the hardware. Now, Tesla uses their lab to refine the software components of their technology to work with a specific neural net architecture in their chips. Their Full Self-Driving (FSD) computer now serves all autopilot features and is ahead of most other auto manufacturers by a wide margin.

This level of invention at Tesla had to happen internally, with alignment between professionals and the company. This could not have happened through collaboration with an agency or third party, not only because of misaligned interests but also because of the company's need for defensibility. For Tesla's Wild product to retain its edge, no one else could poach their ideas and tangible tech. It needed defensibility.

A CTO is Responsible for a Wild Product's Defensibility

Of the three product types, Wild products are the most defensible. What do I mean by defensible? I mean that they are the most competitive in the market and resistant to new competition. When other companies fight for market share, Wild products are best at holding on to what they have. And this provides immense value to your company.

There are three key aspects of product defensibility:

1. **The patents and IP.** Your intellectual property (IP) is heavily protected and if competitors ever want to use your technology, then they'd need to pay licensing fees. Competitors would also need to match your time-to-market and research-and-development resources to compete on your level.

2. **The tech team.** Very few engineers in the world are capable of iterating on the IP you are producing—these engineers make up your tech team. If your competition wants to catch up, it would be very hard to get access to a talent pool like yours.

3. **The product.** Your product embeds a technology that is not easily available to competitors for replication. It would take a significant amount of time and resources to match your technology advancements. In this way, your product has an edge in time and margin when hitting the market.

If your product penetrates the market so it is in the position of having a monopoly, duopoly, or triopoly, you are more or less defended. With majority market share and solid resources, it should be easier to operate and scale your product. If new players want to enter the market, especially a consolidated market, then they'd need significant amounts of capital investment to take a bite off your market share.

Let's dive a bit deeper into the three aspects of product defensibility and how they influence your pick for a CTO.

The Patents and IP

The first layer of defensibility for a Wild product is a patent. When your company has a patent, then you can apply unique IP to your business model. No other company can use your patented designs or code without paying you first. And if you can prove the viability of a patent within your business model, other companies might pay you to license the IP in your patent. A patent can potentially be worth millions of dollars.

The value of your patent gives your business a buffer on your financial margins. It is an extra layer of insurance in case your company goes south. If your product struggles to sell, or if development is behind schedule, then licensing the rights to a patent is an option to gain more funding.

To maximize the value of your patent, your CTO must not only be a technical expert on its contents, but a savvy business person when it comes to communicating the IP's market viability. Your product could be fully functional, proving the value of the patented IP, but if your CTO cannot communicate how this works to potential licensees then you might not make a dime on your IP.

The Tech Team

The second layer of defensibility is the tech team. If you are working on a Wild product, then you need the best engineers in your industry to make your platform competitive. This means your team will be made up of highly specialized individuals. Does this mean you will have to pay them expensive salaries? Yes. But it also means competitors trying to poach your engineers will have to pay them even more.

Many entrepreneurs tend to forget their team members are assets. The team you employ is a big part of the valuation of a company. You could have a dead-end patent and a dumpster fire of a product, but if you have 20 of the best engineers in your industry then you still have a valuable company. Sometimes buyers don't want your company, just the people in it.

So, as your CTO builds your team, don't let them cut costs by hiring junior developers and training them up. Not only will this strategy likely fail, but when it fails, the company will have few assets that could tempt a buyer. To build Wild products, you need *the best* talent on your team.

The Product

The third layer of defensibility is the product itself. If your product works, congratulations! You have a successful technology that no one else in the world has (yet). And, as long as you keep the technology stable and secure, you will likely stay well ahead of your competition. But when it comes to Wild products, the competition doesn't always play fair.

Your product is often the most valuable asset in your company, but it is also the hardest to protect. When you have valuable technology that no one else has, competitors may cheat. The sad reality is that people *do* try to steal tech, and once your tech is out…it's out.

Your CTO is ultimately responsible for the security and

integrity of your product. While they ensure the product's performance and success, they must also structure the team and systems to prevent data leakages.

Imagine if a company like Citadel, a high-frequency trading company moving huge amounts of money around the stock market every day, unintentionally leaked its product. Their entire business model relies on their own, patented trading software to execute the massive number of trades happening in real time. They profit on trades at every moment, which makes them highly attractive to investors. But what if their code was leaked during development? The whole world could have access to their competitive technology overnight, completely diluting interest from investors and tanking the value of their company.

When technology is leaked, it's gone. And the damage is irreparable. So, how does the CTO work to prevent this from happening?

You cannot be 100-percent secure from leaks, but you can have substantial damage limitation. The CTO can structure the team and split up the code so that no one person has access to the entire database. Different cohorts of engineers can be responsible for accessing and improving different parts of the code without ever seeing the whole picture.

In all likelihood, the CTO will be the only person with access to the entire database, but since they will have a large stake in the company it will be in their best interest to keep the product secure. In this spirit, you should *never* outsource the work on critical components of your application to an agency.

The integrity of the product must stay within your company.

Given these unique responsibilities and high stakes, the pool of CTO candidates for a company that is developing a Wild product will indeed be smaller. But finding a "Wild CTO" is not impossible; it just requires a different approach. Again, we are in the Wild West, and there are no paved roads to follow.

How to Find a "Wild CTO"

As mentioned earlier, when you are building a Wild product, as opposed to a Simple or Custom product, your tech partner *must* be an internal CTO. It cannot be an agency, and it certainly cannot be a developer you hope to scale into the role. A big mistake I see people make is to think, "Oh, I will just hire this developer from Google and they'll do all kinds of inventions for me." It's a nice fantasy, but it does not make you competitive.

You must hire a high-performing CTO. Your success depends on this. However, the reality is that the best CTOs and engineers are usually taken! While this makes it easier to identify a CTO (because she or he will likely be currently employed), attracting them to your company is a different challenge. So, what are your options?

The first approach most Wild founders take when securing a CTO is to promote a personal brand that attracts high-quality talent from all over the world. In this case, hiring a CTO comes down to the marketability of the founder. Whether you are a top-tier talent in your industry (on the business side), or a top-tier talent in other business ventures, the opportunity to work with you can be appealing to prospective CTOs.

If the first approach is not an option for you, a second approach is to have enough funding to make an attractive offer to a prospective CTO. If you can raise millions of dollars for your new idea, that will turn heads.

However, after the collapse of FTX and the sentencing of Theranos founder Elizabeth Holmes, investors are more skeptical of charismatic founders with grandiose ideas. This means there is a caveat to having lots of money: your idea must be good *and* feasible. If you haven't done your research and demonstrated a likelihood of success given the right resources, good luck acquiring funding.

Beware the Wizard of Oz Approach

This brings us to a gray area: the "fake it until you make it" approach or, as I like to call it, the Wizard of Oz approach. Everyone wants to follow the Yellow Brick Road to the Emerald City and see the Wizard of Oz. But as soon as the Wizard is revealed to be a fraud, there are consequences. Once an entrepreneur has secured funding and has a plan to phase to a WIld product, they may be tempted to chug along without a CTO for as long as possible, spending capital on other company expenses.

For a clear example of how wrong the Wizard of Oz approach can go wrong, consider Elizabeth Holmes, founder

---

of Theranos. She used the "fake it til you make it" attitude to a fault. The problem was she never made it, and in 2023 a court sentenced her to eleven years in prison for fraud.

Holmes's initial approach to her Wild product was viable. She began with a Simple MVP and used her knowledge of the biotech market and loose plans to phase to a Wild product to attract massive funding. A major problem for Holmes, though, was she didn't use any of the capital to hire a top-tier CTO who could help her plan out how to phase her Simple MVP to the desired Wild product. At a certain point, it was Holmes's responsibility to recognize she couldn't make her tech work. But instead of coming clean, she doubled down, maintaining the illusion of success when no progress had been made. Now she is paying the price while other, better structured biotech companies are picking up where Theranos left off.

To build a Wild product without a CTO is a big gamble. Your CTO is the most crucial and important piece of your business model. My recommendation is to find and hire your CTO first and save your gambling chips for later.

While there are more ways to enter the Wild West of tech and make your product defensible, the approaches we've discussed in this chapter are, in my experience, most common and universal across all Wild products. In the following chapters, we will dig into the specific industries of the Wild product category. We'll see how tokens make blockchain more defensible, why AR/VR products are not as viable as people tend to assume, and the major nuances between different types of AI and how your Wild product might make use of them. Grab your CTO and saddle up!

Chapter 9:
Artificial General Intelligence

The first category of Wild technology we will cover is Artificial Intelligence (AI). Or, as you will come to know it, Artificial General Intelligence (AGI). There is a nuanced difference between the two, and we'll get into that. Startups seem to throw the AI buzzword around at every opportunity. But what is it exactly, beyond ChatGPT, large language models (LLMs) and generative neural networks?

To some, AI might still sound like something out of a science fiction movie (think *Terminator*, or *War Games*), but it's the field where the most groundbreaking innovations are happening right now. This might sound controversial in light of space flight and gene sequencing and other technologies we'll touch on in Chapter 11, but by the end of this chapter you will see how innovations in the field of AI are pushing entire industries in drastic new directions. And it's all happening *now*.

Some may argue the same can be said for any technical innovation, from electricity to microchips. Let me reiterate:

Wild technology must have *practical utility*. It doesn't matter how cool or complex a new technology is, if it doesn't have practical utility to an expansive user base, it is worthless. The business section of your favorite news source might post an article a day on blockchain and cryptocurrency, but how many companies do you know that are actually using blockchain in a way that improves the experience of their users? There are some examples, but not nearly as many as there are for AI.

This chapter will get you up to speed on the essentials of AI and where it is moving—toward AGI. We will review a brief history of AI, discuss AI basics at a technical level, describe the different types of AI, and explore how AI is generally implemented in products. Then, we'll make the distinction between AI and AGI, and discuss how the push for AGI is revolutionizing industries everywhere. By the end of this chapter, you'll see why AGI is worth keeping at the forefront of your mind, no matter what type of product your company is building.

Neural Networks: A Brief History of AI

The concept of AI is rooted in the idea that a machine can function similarly to the neural networks of the human brain. Many people assume this is a relatively new idea, but it was first entertained in the 1960s and 70s, when the scientific community gained a better understanding of the workings of the human brain.

The first computer engineers, armed with the knowledge of

how a complex thinking organ like the human brain worked, were determined to replicate it in machine form. At least in theory, machine neural networks were possible. The biggest problem at the time was that the machinery was massive. To build *machine* neural networks required too much real estate to be feasible. But this soon changed.

As the computing time of processors increased, more powerful AI algorithms were developed. In practice, this meant neural networks (or "neural nets") became possible, allowing computer engineers to experiment with emulating brain activity in machines. This was more than just experimentation, though, because there were potentially powerful practical applications of neural nets—particularly in the field of data science.

The focus of computer engineers in the 1980s and 90s was speed. If engineers could increase computing speed, then computers could perform complex algorithms to solve problems that would otherwise take humans unthinkable hours to perform. The push for better processing speeds intensified in the 1990s with the emergence of parallel computing—the engineering of computers to perform multiple tasks (or multiple parts of one big task) simultaneously. With the mass adoption of parallel computing, complex algorithms got more attention from the data science community.

When we talk about AI, machine learning, data science, and other related fields, the foundational components behind these technologies are neural nets and a diverse landscape of statistical and algorithmic methods. In this sense, AI was first perceived as data science—a means of using advanced algorithms to perform more complex tasks. (This was before supercomputing was a thing.) And from the adoption of neural nets into the field of data science, we trace the evolution of AI as we know it today.

For the purposes of data science, neural nets could solve two big problems: categorization and numerical prediction. Categorization is the function of observing an object's properties and sorting them based on similarities in the data. For example, running a movie script through an AI algorithm to see the movie's genre is an example of categorization.

Numerical prediction has been around longer and is more nuanced. Computers perform numerical prediction when programmers design regression models based on several inputs. This function was possible even on slow processors in the early stages of neural net computing, allowing for the emergence of industries such as weather forecasting.

While neural nets advanced both categorization and prediction abilities in data science, they still had their downsides. The main problem was that neural nets were kind of fixed once they were built—their structure didn't change. This led computer scientists to start thinking about machine learning as the next evolution. The goal was to make neural networks that could optimize and adapt on their own, to keep improving their accuracy over time. Machine learning aimed to take neural nets to the next level.

Researchers were inspired to develop more flexible, adaptable systems for machine learning—systems that could allow a machine to teach itself new things. Machine learning went way beyond static neural nets to the creation of AI that could truly think and learn like humans.

Machine Learning & Generative Neural Nets

When people mention "machine learning" today, they are usually referring to the refining of neural nets to perform categorization and numerical prediction. Rather than perform one function or the other, some neural nets have become so sophisticated that categorization and prediction can happen simultaneously. These neural nets are called generative neural nets.

There are a couple reasons why we see so many different types of neural nets today. One is the increased availability of graphic cards by NVIDIA and AMD. Another is the relatively simple architecture of neural nets. They consist of an activation function, a neural net layer, and the neurons for training the program.

Refining neural nets for categorization and prediction introduced a variety of problems for engineers. Sure, they had the technology, but they still had to put the puzzle pieces together the right way. For example, if they wanted to develop a program that categorized X-ray images of hospital patients, they had to identify precise parameters for every type of problem a patient could have. Even if they were successful in categorizing various types of broken bones, they might face struggle to categorize different types of cancer.

As the field of machine learning has expanded, engineers have introduced more sophisticated techniques to refine the parameters of neural nets based on more dynamic databases. One example of this is the algorithm developed by Cambridge Analytica. Their algorithm used a generative neural net to categorize Facebook users' data, then used that information to predict users' likelihood of being more or less responsive to certain types of posts and advertisements.

This was highly controversial because the algorithm fed users content that validated and polarized extreme opinions. A user susceptible to radically conservative content was fed radically conservative content until they were only consuming radically conservative material. And the same was happening with liberal users, religious users, and any other category that Facebook users could adopt as an identity. In December 2022, Facebook's parent company Meta agreed to pay $725 million to settle a class action lawsuit accusing it of allowing Cambridge Analytica to access and use its user data in this way.

The thought of generative neural nets scraping user data for malicious purposes is scary, and is certainly a problem, but it hopefully won't overshadow the many other positive uses of machine learning.

A more neutral example of what generative neural nets make possible are AI art generators. These generative neural nets use images found in the public domain (usually through Google's database) to create outputs based on relatively broad parameters. It can seem like black magic when you ask an AI art generator for a picture of a cat driving a Lamborghini on the moon and the program outputs exactly that, but this is still a function of categorization and numerical prediction. It generally works like this:

1. The program uses the input ("a cat driving a Lamborghini on the moon") to create the categories that it will sort the data into—a cat, driving, a Lamborghini, on the moon.

2. The program categorizes the data by analyzing the meta tags of all the images in the source database.

3. Based on the images that fit the parameters, the program attributes numerical values to each pixel in each image based on the color.

4. The program then predicts the numerical values of each pixel (read: "the color of each pixel") in an image that fits the parameters of the input.

5. The user observes the program's best prediction of what a cat driving a Lamborghini on the moon looks like based on the images it categorized in the database.

Refining neural nets requires sensitive and conscientious thought. In some cases, machine learning has surpassed human abilities in terms of prediction. Tik-Tok is so successful because it has one of the best (if not the best) neural nets for predicting which content a user will enjoy. No human could best determine what millions of individuals want to see on their screen. But in other cases, machine learning has a long way to go before it can match and surpass human abilities. And perhaps no field is more closely watched than that of natural language processing.

Language Models and the Frontiers of AGI

When we talk about neural nets that can replicate human abilities, we are talking about AGI. And perhaps no human ability is more difficult to replicate than that of human communication. At the forefront of AGI is the development of language models, which seek to understand text in some capacity and also generate it.

Before LLMs, this field was dominated by natural language processors (NLPs). NLPs can recognize sentiments, categorize text, make connections between words and sentences, and create a cohesive structure of language in a mathematical way. For example, companies used NLPs to analyze sentiment within comments on their product feedback across internet. And mathematical connections between words enabled the autocomplete feature in our email. But the innovations that NLPs enabled were just a taste of what was to come.

NLPs remain exciting because they create the building blocks for LLMs, and these models can multiply and extend the connections made by NLPs in a broader context. When this technology is scaled, the number of parameters, connections, and contexts the models can store and analyze make it possible to fill out text in a way that closely mimics human intelligence.

If you haven't experienced working with a LLM yet, you should. Check out ChatGPT, Bard from Google, Claude from

Anthropic. You can have a human-like conversation with what feels like a robot with all-human knowledge.

While the way LLMs work is fascinating, the way they are made is relatively simple. These models just predict the next word based on user input. To train language models, companies like OpenAI, Meta, Google, and Anthropic have taken all text data that is available to them— public and private—and run it through sophisticated machine learning algorithms backed by thousands of modern GPUs.

Open source models and private models

Challenges and opportunities

While companies like Anthropic, OpenAI, Google, and Meta develop and train their own LLMs privately, the open source community is rapidly innovating with publicly available models. And there is a growing divide between advocates for private development and public (open source) development of LLMs. With these two avenues of development comes a handful of challenges and opportunities.

Challenge: Censorship. Companies censor their models for safe use. For example, if you ask an LLM how to break into a car, it will likely not give you much information as the answer is potentially harmful. However, open source models are often uncensored. Any person can access any knowledge and use the knowledge to generate harmful content or take harmful actions. And of course, the model is only as *good* as the individuals and the data that trained it.

Opportunity: Speed. When the first open source LLMs became available, researchers all around the world tinkered with the models and made them more advanced. Companies might employ the top engineers in the world, but the world has numerous engineers who can work together to solve the same problems. Development of LLMs is a race right now, and open source models are catching up with those developed in private.

Challenge and Opportunity: Availability. The majority of open source LLMs are available for use on your own hardware. Some open source LLMs require advanced setup with powerful graphics processing units (GPUs), which can cost more than $10,000, but most of them are compatible with your gaming PC. Some can run on any computer at a decent speed. So far, the most powerful LLMs require expensive setup. This will change, and soon we will be able to access the most powerful LLMs on our phones. The downside to higher availability is an increase in improper use.

Distinguishing AGI from AI

AGI is generative neural nets performing at or above the level of human intelligence, and this is where the field of AI is going. This is where AI has always been going. However, to fully grasp the utility of AGI in the near future we need to distinguish it from AI. And, to distinguish AGI from AI, we need to really understand what AI is.

The term "AI" can often mean anything. Any plain computational application is artificial and has intelligence in some sense, so the term "artificial intelligence" tends to be vague. Even with the implication of "artificial human intelligence," the phrasing is not helpful because "human intelligence" can be easily mimicked.

Alan Turing was a famous mathematician of the 1900s. He helped turn the tides of World War II when he discovered a way to decipher Enigma, the German cypher code used to communicate messages during the war. But Turing's accomplishments go far beyond those in the war. One of his other major contributions is the Turing Test.

In the standard Turing Test suggested in 1950, a person has a verbal conversation with another person and a machine. If the person can't reliably figure out which one is human and which is machine, then the machine is said to pass the Turing Test. Consequently, passing this test has become a major goal in the field of AI. It would mean the machine can communicate so naturally it seems human. However, some criticize the test, saying a machine could trick the person without being truly intelligent. But the Turing Test has still provided an influential way to think about benchmarks for AI capabilities. The test sets a high bar for machines to demonstrate human-level language and reasoning skills.

Today, LLMs can situationally pass the Turing Test, but they cannot do it reliably. Often, the LLM struggles with contextual understanding, maintaining a consistent "personality," and demonstrating the ability to learn in an interaction. Plus, the LLM is only as unbiased as the material it is trained with (and the people who train it). Many users can't tell whether they are interacting with a machine right away, but to most it's clear after some back-and-forth.

Although the Turing Test has long been the standard way to think about AI capabilities, it is not the most advanced benchmark of AI performance today. Rather than picking one benchmark, researchers use a set of tests to measure the performance of AI systems. This set includes, but isn't limited to, the following:

- **Standardized tests.** Tests like the SAT or IQ tests aim to measure general cognitive abilities. AI systems are evaluated based on how well they can perform verbal, mathematical, and reasoning tasks on these tests. Recent LLMs score at or above the human average.

- **Winograd schema challenge.** This assesses common sense reasoning ability using ambiguous pronouns and references that require contextual understanding. Performance remains low for current AI systems.

- **AI2 Reasoning Challenge (ARC) Dataset.** The ARC dataset contains scientific questions aimed at advanced common sense, spatial, temporal, and social reasoning.

- **Multitask benchmarks.** Sets of diverse tasks like language, vision, games, motor control, and physics simulations aim to evaluate general capabilities.

- **Interactive environments.** 3D environments like Minecraft or simulated cities provide interactive settings to evaluate engines on more human-like navigation and mechanics challenges.

- **Turing Test substitutes.** Restricted conversational tests focus on specific social abilities like making jokes, discussing hobbies, or providing empathetic responses.

When to Acquire an AI Tech Expert for Your Product

If you want to build a product that's based on AI technology, do you need an AI tech genius as your CTO? It depends on whether your product is structured around existing models, or if you need to train your own models. If you are building a product around existing LLMs, then it is OK if your CTO has never trained a model. Though, how defensible would your technology be? The application layer of products that are "wrappers" for ChatGPT is fairly thin—any other decent tech team will be able to replicate it in no time when it is based on publicly available models.

Now, when your product is structured around your own AI models, things get interesting. In this type of scenario, you *would* need a CTO who not only knows how to train models (custom LLMs, predictive models, and so on) but who could also manage your company's most valuable asset: DATA.

For example, let's say you're a marketing startup and you now have data for over 100 million users. You are advertising on TV, radio, podcasts, YouTube, and more, and you are getting thousands of views, listens, and clicks. You have data on each individual engaging with your ads. And you have your dev team.

How do you manage the relationship between the developers and the data coming into your organization? Developers need to access the data to work with it, but does it make sense for every developer to have access to all the data? These are questions your CTO must think about and address early on.

If your business model revolves around neural networks, then your data is likely your most valuable asset. But if you don't have someone in your company who is responsible for all the data, then you will have to risk sharing your most valuable asset with a third party. Not ideal.

To keep your data fully internal and secure, your CTO must create systems for sharing portions of the data in house without sharing all of it with any one person. These systems protect the data from leaking. This is a requirement for this kind of business model—you simply need to protect the business.

A common misconception is that the creation of these secure data systems falls under the realm of cybersecurity. This is not quite accurate. Cybersecurity is important, yes, but it's not a CTO responsibility. A more common scenario is for the CTO to communicate with the Chief Information Officer (CIO). The CIO is typically responsible for infrastructure and managing technological risks.

When you're working with massive databases, as AI-based products usually do, the CTO's responsibility is really the management of the data itself. Their efforts to protect this data are focused internally and combined with other organizational efforts. Protecting data from external threats, again, falls to the CIO.

AGI: The Next Frontier of AI

The tech industry is going after AGI right now because its pervasive utility is inevitable. It's not out of the question to think we will achieve AGI within the next decade or two. And when we do, it will be a huge leap forward. We're not there yet, but a lot of progress has been made. OpenAI has ChatGPT, Google has DeepMind, and now even Tesla's robot considered to be competing in this field as well.

AGI is the foremost frontier of Wild technology because the general principle is that once you solve AGI, you can solve everything else. Using the Human Genome Project as a database, AGI could start to uncover possible cures for cancer. It can solve coding errors to clean up technical debt more quickly and synthesize code to make codebases more scalable. It can optimize company meeting schedules and improve communications. It can solve transportation problems and supply chain issues in real time. And so much more.

If realized, AGI could be transformative—for better or worse. Having an AI assistant that turbocharges scientific discovery sounds amazing. But we need to be thoughtful about how quickly this could disrupt economies and jobs. Shifting to using powerful technology requires a shift in mindset about how it's built and deployed.

AGI may still be far off, but this new frontier promises to change everything. With responsible development, it could profoundly enhance our lives. As an entrepreneur, you can play a role in that future by putting AI to work in select areas of your business today.

Chapter 10:
Blockchain

As with most Wild technology, there's a lot of information about blockchain flooding the internet. This can make it seem like anyone interested in learning more about the technology can find what they're looking for, but it's unfortunately not that simple. Blockchain technology is incredibly complex and its functionality differs in nuanced, but significant ways depending on whether it's a private or public blockchain, as we'll discuss in this chapter.

We'll explore what blockchain is and how it can add value to a tech product. We'll also comb through the misconceptions surrounding the technology. You'll get a brief overview of the technology's origins, how the technology works (in general terms...again, it's complex!), and how Bitcoin put it on the map. I'll express why I think blockchain technology has a bad reputation for the wrong reasons. Lastly, I'll discuss Web3 and the future Internet of Things and why, despite some genuine applications of the technology in some industries, most of the excitement surrounding it is hot air and hype.

Before we get into the controversial side of blockchain,

let's start with the basics. What is blockchain? And if it's so overblown, why is it worthy of a full chapter in this book?

Blockchain: What It Is & Why It's Worth Your Attention

Most of the information circulating about blockchain consists of *opinions* about what it can be and should be. Some think it's crypto. Some think it's a scam. Others think it is the basis of Web3…whatever that is. I think it's a push for innovation, and most blockchain experts agree with me. Whether blockchain innovation is good or bad is peripheral. The fact of the matter is that we are living through a time in which the cutting edge of technology in all industries is being reimagined and redefined, and blockchain tends to be at the forefront.

But what is blockchain at a technical level?

To put it as plainly as possible, blockchain is a complex form of cryptography. To be more technically precise, it is a form of decentralized ledger technology. Stay with me…

To clarify, blockchain technology is not new. In the same way that neural networks are not new in the world of AI, the building blocks of blockchain have been around for decades. However, the practical implications of the technology are becoming a reality.

The more blockchain fits itself into industries' business models, the more innovators can imagine further implications for the use of blockchain in different areas. As you will see, some of these implications are causing industries to rethink their value proposition—how their business model serves people. And this is all due to one central facet of blockchain technology:

Blockchain assumes decentralization

To explain the function of decentralization, I'll use a quick analogy. Imagine you live in a small fishing town. Every morning the fishermen come in and deliver their catch to the fishmonger. As they hand over their catch, the fish are weighed and the net total is reported in the fishmonger's ledger. At the end of the week, the fishmonger's accountant pays out each fisherman based on the numbers reported in the ledger.

In theory, there is nothing wrong with this system. In practice, though, several things tend to go wrong. Some fishermen might threaten the fishmonger to rig the scales in their favor. Other fishermen might threaten the accountant to fix the book retroactively and inflate their payout number. And if the fishmonger or the accountant start bending the rules, the remaining honest fishermen might notice something's wrong. If all the fishermen discovered the rules of this simple system are rigged, how can any of them ever trust the system?

The system described in this analogy is called a centralized ledger system. This means there is one ledger, and the whole system is founded on the integrity of that ledger. If the ledger is messed with at any point, the whole system breaks down. Now, can you start to see how *decentralization* changes the system?

In an effort to reintroduce integrity to the ledger system, every fisherman starts recording all the fish weights in their *own personal ledger*. Further, the fishermen appoint a board of record keepers. This board is present every morning as the fishermen weigh their catches. The catches are also weighed by some of the board members themselves. Then, every member of the board records the weight of each fisherman's catch in their own separate ledger.

At the end of the week, all board members submit a copy of their ledgers to the accountant and a copy to all the fishermen. If there are any discrepancies, the accountant or the fishermen can either assume, *Oh, only one ledger reports a different number so maybe that one was just a misprint.* Or, *It doesn't look like the ledgers are in agreement on my catch. Maybe I should talk to the board to find out what happened.*

With this decentralized ledger system, any and all discrepancies can be handled with transparency. The result is that all members of the system are incentivized to be honest because cheating is more obvious and requires conspiring with every member of the board to rig the system. Not impossible, but certainly much more difficult.

Blockchain technology is essentially this decentralized ledger system at massive scale.

In most Western industries, the systems (and thus the technology) are centralized. The most obvious example is the finance industry. In most economies today, currencies are regulated by governments and central banks.

In the U.S., government institutions are set up to monitor

the dollar and keep the economy healthy. The Department of the Treasury manages and regulates the printing and distribution of coins and dollar bills. The Federal Trade Commission regulates the buying and selling of public companies to protect consumers. In addition to these two bodies, a half-dozen other federal institutions coordinate to ensure the dollar is protected from fraud, illegal printing, uncontrollable inflation, and more.

At the consumer level, people interact with private financial institutions to manage and protect their money. Private banks, such as Bank of America, JP Morgan Chase, and Wells Fargo, provide consumers with a centralized system for managing and insuring their finances. And there are a lot of benefits to working in this kind of centralized system, because when problems arise, the bank shares responsibility for dealing with the problems. If someone hacks your account and illegally transfers your money, you can open a case with your bank and they will reimburse you while they work to get the money back. This doesn't mean the centralized systems are perfect, but they have proven good enough for the masses for centuries.

For the longest time, finances have revolved around centralized monetary systems, so it can be hard to imagine what decentralized monetary systems look like. We won't get into ICOs (Initial Coin Offering) or cryptocurrency or investment opportunities, but we can ask the question: What do decentralized financial systems mean for consumers? To help answer this question, we can look to how innovators are thinking about blockchain, and its current (and possible future) impact on industries around the globe.

Consumer Utility, Cryptography, and the Origin of Cryptocurrency

What benefit does blockchain technology provide to consumers? If you start with this question, then you're already thinking ahead of most other entrepreneurs and investors. In the last four to five years, a lot of companies started to include blockchain as part of their spiel—especially in the VC space—but few people have managed to competently answer the question.

In your product, is blockchain a real utility? Why is it in your product? What functionality does it add? Is there a unique value that it brings? Or is blockchain just a sexy thing to put in a pitch deck and hopefully add millions of dollars to your company's valuation?

In my experience, it's common for entrepreneurs to cite their product's use of blockchain as a way to raise more capital without thinking about its real utility. Many do the same thing with AI but, because AGI is closer than most people realize, AI technology often brings actual utility to a product (for example, business automation). But blockchain, if you can believe it, is a bit more complicated. In some cases, it has utility, but in many cases it's fancy deadweight. And this can be quite controversial.

Why the controversy? Well, blockchain has a bit of a reputation and this muddies people's understanding of what the technology is. So, let's rewind the clock a little bit. I won't cover the entire history of blockchain (that would be mind-numbing), but I will quickly summarize the fundamentals of the technology and how Bitcoin eventually landed blockchain on the public scene.

At a technical level, what made blockchain possible was innovation in cryptography. This innovation happened more than 40 years ago. In the years leading up to Bitcoin, and in the years since, incredible innovations continue to take place with the cryptographic code that lays the groundwork for blockchain technology. For software engineers, these innovations are mind blowing.

To keep our technical review as simple as possible, we'll focus on three things: **public keys, private keys**, and **wallets**. Understanding these three things will help you understand how data is stored on the blockchain. It will also help you understand blockchain's application for attributing ownership of digital assets—one of the technology's primary utilities. You own a digital asset by having a pair of public and private keys, and signed transactions on a blockchain. In order to have these three things, you must have a wallet. Ok, I know this is getting confusing, so let's rewind.

For blockchain transactions, your private and public keys are stored in your wallet. Your wallet can be a physical hard drive, a flash drive, your computer, or even your phone. It depends on the blockchain.

Let's say someone is sending you a Bitcoin. They can send it to your wallet using their private key and your public key. What you receive is a transaction signed by their private key (although you can only see their public key) that designates the Bitcoin to your public key. And now that the Bitcoin is in your wallet, you can only spend it with your private key. You now own the Bitcoin.

To be clear, you didn't have to do anything. The other person signed the transaction to your public key with their private key, which means the whole database can see that you now own the Bitcoin (not you the person, but you as the owner of the public key). And via the transaction you now have a record in your ledger of this transaction and every transaction of the Bitcoin that came before it, all the way back in time to the original owner. And you own the Bitcoin until you sign a transaction with your private key attributing the Bitcoin to someone else's public key.

This might sound relatively straightforward. Essentially, on a decentralized digital ledger, computers (observers, or "fishermen") can verify every single transaction without the need for a central authority (a bank, or a "fishmonger"). But the technical behind-the-scenes of blockchain technology is incredibly complicated. If you're interested in getting into the weeds, I recommend reading Satoshi Nakamoto's white paper. It lays out the technical fundamentals for storing data in a *decentralized* database, and how a decentralized database can make data immutable. In other words, people could own the data. If the data exists on a publicly available platform, then anyone can observe the current state of the data at any time. In this case, the data is posted transactions. In practical terms, the platform works like a ledger system.

If all data is public, then how do you structure the database so that the data is protected to the degree that it is effectively unalterable? In other words, how do you create a database that prohibits data from being changed, even by admins? In the case of Bitcoin, this means assuring that the data is of the highest integrity. This includes data that identifies not just the owners of coins, but the previous owners and the exact times of transactions. It's a valid question. Thankfully, the cryptographic innovations behind blockchain address this question.

Crypto Controversy and the Practicality of Decentralized Currencies

From the moment Nakamoto's white paper was released in 2008, Bitcoin (and cryptocurrency in general) was laced with controversy. It didn't help that "Satoshi Nakamoto" was a pseudonym for an unknown person, or group of people. Further, while the data was publicly available, any user could manage anonymity by using cryptic public keys. This, to be blunt, opened the door for money to move a bit more freely through unregulated markets (black markets). But we won't go down that rabbit hole. The fact of the matter is that while the tangible value of Bitcoin has always been volatile and imprecise, the blockchain technology works more or less as intended.

What many people don't realize is that Bitcoin is open source, meaning that anyone can clone it however many times they want and start their own version. Some people have done this as a joke and made millions of dollars (Dogecoin). While others have taken the blockchain and optimized the technology for consumer utility (Ethereum). But if Bitcoin, Dogecoin, and Ethereum all use similar fundamentals, how is the value of each coin different?

What makes Bitcoin—and any cryptocurrency—valuable is the *immutability* of the data (or, its integrity). And what makes the data immutable is something called consensus mechanism. The big picture idea behind consensus is this: When new blocks get populated (meaning a new transaction takes place or a new crypto asset is created), someone has to verify those blocks. This is analogous to the board of record keepers in the fishermen's ledger system. In the case of Bitcoin, these record keepers are called "Bitcoin miners" which perform heavy crypto computations on specialized hardware. And this mining process is also decentralized.

The incentives for being a record keeper (a miner) on a blockchain are lucrative. Miners fight for the right to verify new blocks because those who succeed earn a little cryptocurrency as a reward for the work. But the work, to put it lightly, is insanely difficult.

In the case of Bitcoin, mining requires a lot of computing power. So much so that 0.5% to 1% of all global electricity goes into mining Bitcoin. This is nuts, but from a technical point of view it makes sense. The immutability aspect of the cryptocurrency (and thus its tangible value) relies on the integrity of the consensus mechanism, and if it lacks integrity then the database won't be as immutable.

However, there are other consensus mechanisms that don't require a lot electricity. Ethereum recently transitioned to a different verification process that uses 99% less energy than

Bitcoin's. And if cryptocurrencies can continue to solve these practical problems, then their utility for consumers may become a reality.

On the Horizon: Smart Contracts and NFTs

Even as cryptocurrencies aren't ready for widespread adoption as currency, there are other innovative uses of blockchain technology. Consider this scenario: If you have a database of immutable information, you can not only store who owns a portion of an asset, but you can also store programs. Further, you can store the result of execution of those programs. So, participants can build mini applications on the blockchain. These mini applications are called "smart contracts."

The first blockchain to spearhead experimentation with smart contacts was Ethereum, when they enacted the widespread use of non-fungible tokens (NFTs). An NFT is a digital asset built onto the blockchain. It can be anything. An image, a song, a .zip file, even a newspaper article. They can be transferred the same way crypto coins are transferred (owner uses their private key to assign the asset to another person's wallet via their public key). However, most NFT owners want something in exchange for their creation, and not just from the first transaction but from every subsequent transaction. This is where smart contracts come into play.

Any user on the blockchain can register their own smart contract. These contracts can even have their own data storage and a little bit of functionality. For example, the creator of an NFT can write into the initial smart contract that every time the specified NFT is transferred from one wallet to another for Ethereum, a percentage of the transacted Ethereum goes to their wallet. In other words, they take a cut of every sale of their NFT, not just the first one. (This is revolutionary for the traditional art market, where art often sells for higher prices on secondary markets, yet artists receive no kickbacks.)

From this small application on Ethereum, bigger ideas have been born. Multimedia artists designed contracts that gave the first buyers of their NFTs special access to secret projects. For example, a musician might release 100 copies of their upcoming album's artwork as NFTs, and the first people to buy those NFTs get a private link to the musician's demo set list for the upcoming album. Or perhaps the first-time buyers receive a one-time-use passcode to an online chatroom with the musician. Or a coupon that can be redeemed for free VIP tickets to any of the musician's upcoming concerts. Once you start thinking, the ideas are seemingly endless.

But we wouldn't be talking about cryptocurrency if there weren't controversy. The main caveat to all of these cool ideas is that they rely on the crypto coins being exchanged for digital assets to have tangible, real-world value. At the time of writing, one Ethereum coin is worth just over US$1,500. But where does this value come from? Not from the decentralized community that hosts the blockchain, but from a exchange markets: both centralized and decentralized.

Trading crypto on centralized markets can work, but when

it doesn't work, it's messy. You might be familiar with the FTX fiasco, but what exactly was going on behind the scenes that made such a mess to begin with? To understand this, we must first understand what needs to happen for this centralized exchange model to work. And there are examples of it working.

When a centralized institution takes people's real-world money to trade digital assets on the blockchain, there are a handful of boxes that must be checked. The institution has to take care of their infrastructure, security, exchange mechanics, accounting, and so on. And it all has to be top notch. A company like Coinbase appears to be solid in all these regards. They have legal compliance, secure technology, and a respectable amount of capital; everything you could want in a business. FTX, though, didn't seem to have checked any of these boxes.

When all of your transactions are centralized, you have to keep track of them. You have to keep a tight ledger. FTX not only omitted a ledger of their transactions, but they weren't even keeping track of their employees! When Sam Bankman-Fried was arrested, he had no idea how many people worked for him at his own company. All he knew was that people were investing their money in FTX and employees were playing with the money on public (and maybe private) blockchains. When authorities looked behind the curtain, all the investors realized that there was no way of knowing whether their investments had increased or decreased in value. So, the reliability of digital assets holding real-world value tanked, meaning that everyone essentially lost money. A lot of money.

There is an alternative to trading digital assets on centralized exchanges, and this is a decentralized exchange—a way to exchange digital assets on one or even between blockchains. I find the concept of DEXs (Decentralized Exchanges) fascinating, even with all controversy in blockchain. If you are brave enough for this rabbit hole, lookup Uniswap Protocol. It is one of the largest decentralized protocols for trading any asset against each other on blockchain. But it's time to take this conversation beyond the bounds of cryptocurrency.

Improving Industries with Blockchain and the Web3 Dream

In Nakamoto's white paper, the idea of blockchain was just laid out for currency, but it's since been discovered that this concept of storing data in a decentralized digital ledger system has a broad span of applications in other industries. In terms of how blockchain technology can be implemented, there are three general categories of thought. The first is that all industries everywhere will become synthesized under a new blockchain-based Internet called Web3 (I don't think so). The second category of thought is that blockchain should be approached as an excellent add-on to existing industries, but not as a new foundation for all industries to be rebuilt on. Finally, there is a third group of innovators who are aspiring to invent new industries altogether on the blockchain. While I certainly have my bias, all three categories are worth exploring in the spirit of thinking big and pushing innovation forward.

The first category of thought behind the future of blockchain revolves around this thing called "Web3" (or "Web 3.0"). Web3 is the term used to refer to the supposed third iteration of the World Wide Web. Most people don't realize we are currently on Web2, the second iteration of the web. We are. And depending on who you ask, Web3 is either on the horizon, decades away, a fantastical dream, or already here.

But what is Web3? (Or what *will* it be if it comes to exist?) If Web2 is an interconnected media, then Web3 will be a decentralized internet. Right now, all information on the internet is stored on servers all over the world. If one server location goes down, that portion of the internet will cease to function unless there is cross-zone availability servers ready to back things up. (This is the infrastructure we covered in Chapter 7.)

Web3, however, would strive to make every server a balanced piece of the puzzle. Every computer would share responsibility for keeping this new internet functional, immutable, and secure. Here's my take: The Web3 concept is a bit of a pipe dream. Don't get me wrong, I love sophisticated technology. But decentralizing the entire World Wide Web would require a level of coordination that is improbable. We're talking about overhauling the infrastructure of a network with billions of websites and trillions of pages. Even if we could wave a magic wand and make it technically feasible, does anyone seriously think the major players who control the internet today would voluntarily decentralize their power? Highly unlikely.

I'm sure the blockchain evangelists have good intentions with their vision of a utopian decentralized internet. But we've got to focus on practical solutions that solve real problems people have today. And people aren't exactly clamoring for a Web3 right now. For most, the internet works fine as it is. Unless there's a clear, game-changing reason to rebuild the foundations of the internet, upending its infrastructure seems like a waste. We don't need to decentralize just for decentralization's sake.

However, from a security standpoint, decentralization could actually be a great thing! Most people may not want access to all of their information on the internet to be contingent on their ability to keep their private key secure, but in certain scenarios and in certain industries this kind of security can be a great feature. This brings us to the second category of thought surrounding the future of blockchain: that it will become an add-on to existing industries.

Many people cringe at the idea of a new internet on blockchain (myself included), but the incredible capabilities of the technology are still worth consideration. I am not convinced that Web3 is the next sequential progression in web technology. There was a time I heard from startup founders every week at pitch meetings something along the lines of, "Oh, we can build this product on Web2 and transition to Web3 in a year…" But this assumes the development of the web is sequential. That's not how I see it.

As far as I can tell, Web2 is the internet, and that's it. Period. No products are going onto the darknet, or another decentralized network, but rather onto cloud storage (probably Amazon cloud) using email and types of Web2 internet technology. In the second category of thought, Web3 is the attempt to use the blockchain component as an *add-on*, not a replacement, to existing technology. As long as the addition has utility, it's good, but it's not a new (or next) web.

Many people are integrating blockchain technology to innovate existing products and business models. Some companies are already making good use of this technology as an add-on to their current infrastructure. Private hospitals, firms, and corporations are all finding ways to optimize aspects of their business with decentralized digital ledgers. From solving supply chain problems to speeding up customer service to simply improving data security, blockchain is proving to have some utility.

In order to apply the security and functionality of blockchain technology as an add-on, companies are building their own private blockchains. Every blockchain mentioned so far (Bitcoin, Ethereum, Dogecoin) is public. On public blockchains, the data is visible to everyone, meaning anyone can access and copy the data at any time. But nobody does this because the public blockchain databases are massive and immutable. Still, it is technically possible for someone to download the entire Bitcoin database—all the transactions that have happened over the years with every detail on the transactions (with only a few exceptions). Unrealistic, but technically possible. This is not the case with private blockchains.

Private blockchains bring the same decentralization component of public blockchains, but with the caveat that the database is not available to the public. The private blockchain has a closed, authorized network of participants. This makes the technology more appealing for parties that would need to exchange private information—banks, governments, supply chains, hospitals, law firms, and so on.

For example, on a private blockchain you could have an insurance carrier requesting your private records from a hospital. Assuming you are a participant on this hospital's private blockchain, you could use a public key to give the insurance company temporary access to view your private information on the blockchain. The blockchain would then record the fact that the insurance company viewed your information, and for how long, before closing access to your information once again. The insurance company receives the information they need to file your claim, and your confidential files remain secure and unchanged on the hospital's database.

In other words, all information and the use of information on private blockchains is both secure and fully auditable.

Building the infrastructure to make their databases truly decentralized is a significant investment, but some companies are proving it's a worthy investment. One of the clearest examples of this is Walmart's move to put their supply chain on a private, decentralized digital ledger system.

In 2020, Walmart Canada collaborated with Hyperledger Fabric, a subsidiary of the non-profit Linus Foundation. Hyperledger Fabric would provide Walmart with the infrastructure needed for a private blockchain. But what motivated this massive shift in the first place? It all started with a batch of bad produce.

When Walmart Canada discovered that one of the farms

they source their greens from had a pest infestation, they had no way of quickly tracking which bags of greens were carrying the pest on store shelves.[1] So, to mitigate risk, they pulled *all* bags from their store shelves. This alone was a costly hit, but the pain only worsened as they struggled to track other shipments in the supply chain carrying the pest. Weeks passed, and the problem solved itself as all bags of greens in Walmart's inventory expired. When all was said and done, the company lost millions of dollars in expired inventory, and all because they couldn't get reliable information fast enough.

Once Walmart Canada was set up on their new private blockchain, all their inventory could be tracked from farm to store shelf in near real time. Each bag of greens carried a barcode and each time the barcode was scanned the database was updated with a new block of code—similar to how a transaction would take place on a public blockchain. So, the next time an infestation broke out at one of the source farms, Walmart was able to find out in less than two days exactly which bags in which stores and in which freight containers needed to be thrown out. If anything, there was nothing more than a minor hiccup in their supply chain, where months before the same problem had dealt the company a heavy blow.

Companies aren't the only organizations making use of private blockchains. In 2012, Estonia became the first country to fully integrate blockchain technology into its systems.[2] Even

---

1 https://www.hyperledger.org/learn/publications/dltlabs-case-study
2 https://e-estonia.com/wp-content/uploads/2020mar-nochang-es-faq-a4-v03-blockchain-1-1.pdf

before Nakamoto's white paper was released in 2008, Estonia had been testing blockchain technology for security purposes. For Estonia, 2007 was a brutal year. The country experienced foreign cyberattacks and the government needed a solution to protect itself and its citizens' data from enemy states. It chose to integrate KSI Blockchain technology, a private blockchain technology also used by NATO and the U.S. Department of Defense.

The utility of having an entire country on a blockchain is that every change in data is instantly detected and recorded. If your personal information is accessed or updated (name, address, car registration, passport photo), the blockchain records exactly who accessed or changed it, when, and sometimes where. It's a fascinating experiment, and while this might not be an ideal solution for all countries, it seems to be making a lot of sense for Estonia.

When treating blockchain technology as an add-on to existing infrastructure (and not a replacement), we can see how some companies are finding genuine utility in the technology. Some companies have already integrated blockchain technology without their users being aware. For example, most Reddit account holders are unaware they have a crypto wallet. However, this is again a centralized way of owning data. Reddit, Coinbase, and banks own your private keys, which means the system is not decentralized by any means.

Whatever you believe about decentralized systems, it's worth noting how the use and development of blockchain technology is pushing industries to innovate. Blockchain forces people to think about ways to update and improve existing business models. And getting people to think differently about the world's problems is rarely a bad thing.

And now we address the third camp of people who hope to invent new industries altogether with blockchain. Earlier in this chapter, we discussed the emergence of NFTs as a solution to the problem most people have with "owning" a digital asset on the internet. The problem is that if an asset is digital, then it can just be copied, right? Well, yes. But as long as you have your private key, you can prove ownership of a precise digital asset. People can still copy it, but they cannot prove ownership as long as they do not have your private key.

In a sense, this *feeling* that you own a digital asset is artificial. But the feeling still has value. Millions of dollars of value depending on who you ask. The concept of owning digital assets is an industry. And the biggest market share is in the gaming sector.

The push for new blockchain industries in the world of gaming has its own controversy. Most of the major gaming platforms (such as Blizzard) forbid users from selling their in-game data or game disks to others. I doubt users would go to prison if they sold their data, but they are technically violating Blizzard's terms of agreement if they sell their *World of Warcraft* avatar's gold coins for real money. This is because Blizzard technically owns that avatar and those gold coins. However, the idea of owning digital assets on a blockchain can change all of this.

A gaming environment on a blockchain could become its

own marketplace because, on a blockchain, there would be no debate regarding who owns what. This means there is a future where users legally transfer ownership of digital assets in video games—the same way you would buy, sell, or rent something on Ebay or Craigslist. So, in a blockchain video game, users will own their avatar and resources as NFTs. They can then lend or sell their assets to other users in exchange for other NFTs (or cryptocurrency) via smart contracts.

If users can buy, sell, and rent digital assets in a video game, then there's no reason why similar marketplaces can't pop up elsewhere. People are already experimenting with ways to lease audio tracks or loops on blockchain marketplaces for music sampling. This idea almost certainly extend to stock images and video, software programming, and even digital creative services sites. However, making idea into practical product is especially hard with such Wild technology.

Getting Hands-On with Blockchain: Obstacles and Opportunities

No matter which camp of thought you identify with, it's worth keeping an eye on blockchain as people continue to experiment and innovate with the technology. However, if you are thinking about actually building something with blockchain, there are significant obstacles worth considering.

The biggest obstacle to blockchain's future is the lack of fraud protection and recourse. In a centralized system, if a user thinks they are the victim of fraudulent activity, then they can file a claim with their bank or provider and work to solve the problem. But in a decentralized system, if you are the victim of fraud then you're completely out of luck—there is no central institution to make your case with or to recover stolen funds. This lack of consumer protection is a dealbreaker for average users.

Another major blockade is the terrible usability that comes with blockchain's reliance on private keys and digital wallets. Managing cryptographic keys and remembering passwords is a usability nightmare for non-technical users. If you lose your private key, you lose access to your assets permanently with no recovery option. No one wants the hassle of securing their private keys like they are precious jewels. The average consumer will never accept or understand this.

With these huge obstacles in mind, I advise most entrepreneurs to avoid building products on blockchain technology entirely. The only scenarios where it may make sense is if your industry absolutely requires the tamper-proof data integrity that comes with decentralization, and if you can implement it in a private setting with some controls in place. Outside of these niche use cases, integrating blockchain into your consumer product will likely create more problems than it solves.

Perhaps in the future, using crypto will be as easy as swiping a credit card. But we aren't there yet—not even close. That's why building a product to leverage cryptocurrencies as payment rails is fraught with friction. For now, entrepreneurs are better off treating crypto as a speculative digital asset rather than real-world currency.

Chapter 11:
Wild Innovation

In terms of Wild technology, there is some incredible innovation taking place, but most of it won't have practical utility in the near future. Similar to AI and blockchain, you likely won't be incorporating the tech in this chapter into your business. However, these categories have more innovation to come, so it's important to be aware of the practical utility of each, and the potential future effects.

In this chapter, we will cover some of the major categories of Wild tech innovation, but we will approach them as trends to watch instead of deep rabbit holes to fall down. The first three categories we will look at are metaverse systems, virtual reality (VR), and augmented reality (AR). While closely related, these are all different technologies. That's correct, the metaverse is not synonymous with VR. We'll also look at quantum computing—really cool technology, but also the biggest threat to blockchain security. Finally, we will touch on gene editing and DNA sequencing. We'll cover that category last because, while it has perhaps the most promising practical utility to the future of humanity, its full potential will rely on the successful integration of many of the other Wild technologies covered in this book.

First, let's discuss metaverse systems because while they're known for being fun, they're also controversial.

Metaverse Systems, Virtual Reality, and Augmented Reality

Similar to Bitcoin, cryptocurrency, and blockchain, there is a lot of excitement in the public sphere around metaverse, VR, and AR. The three are often conflated, even though they are different terms. Yes, there is some overlap, but before we get too far into the weeds, let's clarify some things.

First, metaverse is a term used to refer to a digital space where users can socialize and interact, but there is one key mechanic: in a metaverse, users can interact with the platform to build automated tasks and create their own personalized environments and experiences. Without this key mechanic, the digital space is just another social media platform—even if the platform is in VR.

However, VR is a different type of technology. VR technology gives users a fully immersive visual, auditory, and spatial experience. These are the packages including headsets, headphones, and handheld paddles that give people the experience of fighting off an alien invasion at the top of Mount Everest or exploring shark-infested shipwrecks at the bottom of the ocean.

There is likely a future where VR combines with metaverse systems—which is what Facebook's parent company, Meta, is banking on—but more on that in a minute.

The last technology that gets jumbled together with metaverse and VR is AR. This technology can sometimes be dismissed as a poor man's VR, but AR is cool in its own right and has tons of practical utility. Most people think it's only good as a gimmick for Snapchat filters and Pokémon Go. However, as you'll see, there are plenty of industries that can make good use of technology that interprets and outputs visual data that interacts with real-world inputs in real time.

Between these three Wild technologies, there is a lot to cover. And there is quite a bit of overlap. To paint the best picture of what they are and what their utility can be in the future, let's quickly review the origin of it all: a clunky little video game called Minecraft.

Minecraft and My First Metaverse

For me — inventor of the metaverse is one person, the creator of Minecraft. Markus "Notch" Persson developed Minecraft using the Java coding language and made the game public in 2009. In the game, players control blocky avatars that can explore the world, gather resources, fight monsters, and (most importantly) build. Build what? *Anything the player wants.*

I love gaming, was not crazy about Minecraft, but my kids loved Minecraft a lot. At one point, I was living in New York, while my kids were overseas. We would spin up Minecraft server and play in this virtual worlds together creating whatever we wanted from building materials gathered around the virtual world in different setting. How that is not a whole meta universe where connections between people possible?

Minecraft players effectively discovered that it was possible to recreate the behavior of a transistor in the game. And when that is possible, you can create a computer on top of it. Suddenly, there was so much more for players to do in the game besides building homes and fighting monsters. They could automate the mining of in-game resources, and they could also create cars to automatically drive resources from their mines to another location. They could build a castle with trap doors, or they could build an apartment complex with a fully functional elevator. They could build a catapult, a Ferris wheel, or a fully automated self-parking garage.

This core mechanic was not a central feature of the game, it was more of an add-on, but it grew in popularity. It wasn't long before people started creating in-game services and unique experiences around this core mechanic. We're talking about Minecraft escape rooms, maximum-security island prisons, and even one fan-favorite game called Bed Wars. In Bed Wars, players hide their bed on an island, protect it, and then try to find the beds of other people. It's a nutty idea, but Minecraft is now filled with fun and nutty ideas that anyone can engage with. And if a player doesn't like those ideas, they can create their own.

So, in this sense, Minecraft became the first metaverse. Players can use one in-game avatar character to traverse the world and play a number of different types of games, and simultaneously socialize with real human beings via the Internet.

And so, Minecraft quickly became the most popular game in the world. The bright people at Microsoft noticed this and proceeded to buy the game from Notch for about $1 billion.

But enough about the first metaverse. What about the *best* metaverse? How has this technology developed and what is its future? Who's leading the charge? All good questions, and for answers we must look at three more companies: Roblox, Epic Games, and Meta.

Roblox is perhaps the most directly comparable game, or gaming platform, to Minecraft. The idea behind Roblox was essentially to take the core mechanic that made Minecraft so popular and establish an entire gaming platform around that functionality. So, while Minecraft has monsters to run from or kill, Roblox has whatever its users dream up and develop.

Released in 2006, Roblox is about the same age as Minecraft, but it has way more users. As of 2021, Minecraft had an estimated 93 million users, a drop from its peak of 131 million users in 2020. Roblox, on the other hand, has approximately 202 million users today. Perhaps there is something to be said for offering users a platform they can fully customize.

To be clear, Roblox does not have the exact same functionality as Minecraft. Users do not mine resources to build from. Instead, the Roblox platform itself is fully customizable. Users can create simple, unique experiences for other users to engage with—like mazes where you run from giant pigs and rats, or a universe where you collect coins to progress to different levels and craft pets. Given the amount of customization offered to users, Roblox is one platform to follow as metaverse systems develop.

Another metaverse system that is often overlooked is the game Fortnite, by Epic Games. Epic Games is a gaming studio that produced the Unreal Engine, a powerful gaming engine used to build phenomenal games. We're talking about games with high-quality graphics, fast gameplay speeds, and expansive worlds. Games like Fortnite.

Like Minecraft, Fortnite has its own central gameplay and storyline, but it also allows users to take their character and their character's weapons and create other experiences on the platform. So, Fortnite also offers the key central mechanic in an interactive digital universe, allowing users to customize their own gameplay within the game. Hence, it can be argued that Fortnite is a metaverse system.

As of 2020, Fortnite had 350 million registered users. This is perhaps unsurprising given that the game is free through Epic Games and there are more than 500 million Epic Games accounts.[3] There are in-game purchases for cosmetics, but you don't need to spend money to play and win the game or explore the world. It's likely that many players use the game to simply socialize via their avatars with no goal or purpose in mind, doing or creating whatever they want. It will be interesting to see what Epic Games does with this metaverse system moving forward.

And then...there's Meta's metaverse.

In the technical sense, the Meta metaverse which has

---

3 https://www.engadget.com/epic-games-accounts-500-million-165908445. html

evolved as an offshoot from Facebook (now Meta) is a step forward from the world of Minecraft. Meta is developing their metaverse with the intention of establishing it on a VR platform. This is not to say Microsoft, Roblox, and Epic Games can't follow suit with their games and platforms, but Meta is working hard to stay ahead of the curve here. However, this is purely in the technical sense.

In a practical sense, Meta's metaverse is a step backward. This is because (at the time of writing) their metaverse lacks the core mechanic that Minecraft, Roblox, and Fortnite thrive on. In Meta's metaverse, there is no way for users to customize the environment and create unique experiences. Their metaverse is just a social space for people to gather in general. You create an account…you're there…so what? Meta avatars don't even have legs for crying out loud!

To be fair, Meta's metaverse only launched in 2022 and the biggest concern right now is the development of the VR component. The core functionality of a metaverse system may not exist right now, but it might be incorporated in the future. Combined with the fact that the platform is (currently) free, there might be reason to think that Meta's metaverse could be the first VR metaverse system, and that would be a significant milestone—one worth keeping an eye out for.

Metaverses on their own don't have an obvious practical utility, besides being beloved by millions of users. They are a virtual place where people from all over the world can connect by competing or working together. It's possible there is untapped power in mobilizing millions of users to solve real-world problems. But for now, metaverses are pushing development in two other technologies: VR and AR.

Let's talk about the VR component and its oft-overlooked, more promising little cousin, AR.

Virtual Reality and Augmented Reality

It can be argued that VR and AR are two sides of the same coin, but you won't find me making that argument. This is because, when the VR headsets come off and you take a look around, you'll see that VR has a small user base while AR has managed to land itself *everywhere*. Why is this?

The idea of being instantly transported to another dimension where you can travel the world, fight aliens, or play tennis all from the comfort of your living room sounds sexy. And VR offers users a litany of unique experiences. The technology is pretty darn cool and fun to play around with…at least for a little while.

I own an Oculus Headset—the device Meta is banking on launching their metaverse—but after 30 minutes of wearing it, I get dizzy. So dizzy that I felt like throwing up. And I am not alone here.

About 30 percent of users report feeling dizzy or nauseous after just 30 minutes of wearing VR headsets. And yet, I cannot tell you how many non-technical founders come to me each week trying to pitch an idea involving a VR metaverse on blockchain. It can all sound really cool and exciting until a third of your users feel like puking after a half-hour and another handful have lost their private keys.

We must return to the same question driving all Wild technology innovation: What is the **practical utility** of the technology? What is the practical utility of VR to users? Why would the masses line up for this product? A lot of investors seem to be lining up, but they are banking on a trend, a concept, a blank canvas. Maybe they know something I don't—maybe Meta will build on top of this technology (and I hope they do), but from the outside looking in, it doesn't seem encouraging.

This is hard for me to write as a technical person. I want to be sensitive to the brilliant minds developing this highly innovative technology. But it honestly doesn't matter how cool it all is if there is no utility. Or, at least highly limited utility.

VR may have some utility when it comes to simulating high-stakes scenarios in secure environments for training purposes. Military personnel can train for special ops or practice routine (albeit still life-and-death) scenarios. First responders can practice responding to uncertain situations. Surgeons can practice a number of surgeries without needing a number of cadavers. Even the film and television industry is investing heavily in VR—check the behind-the-scenes on *The Mandalorian* or *Avatar: The Way of Water*. The list of niche utilities for VR is lengthy. But what would make the average person line up for VR products over other products?

The reality is that there is not a long line of consumers for VR products, but there is a huge market for AR.

There was a buzz of AR excitement a few years ago when the Pokémon Go app launched. It turns out the technology has found its way into a number of popular products like Instagram, Snapchat, and TikTok. Beyond the sphere of social media platforms, AR is also finding its way into apps with more practical utility.

One of the many companies that had foresight on this technology was Apple. The company has cracked into AR by developing iPhone features that allow users to point a phone camera and see a superimposed image on their screen, on top of the real-world image. And, most of the time, the superimposed image has functionality. For example, while there are apps that can scan barcodes and QR codes for you, iPhone users can simply turn on their phone's camera, point it at the code, and immediately be prompted to open the link assigned to the code.

Further, Apple also developed a software development kit (SDK) for AR developers that is simple to use. This means any developer team can license the SDK to develop an app that uses AR technology for an Apple product. However, one of the most commonly used functionalities of this SDK is also one of the most controversial.

Face mask apps are incredibly popular but have a fair share of negative press. These are apps that can track faces on camera and show augmentations on the screen—a dog nose, bunny ears, a halo, or devil horns. All of this happens in real time. This technology opens the door for fun applications, but also some nefarious backend activity.

Apps that superimpose graphics over a user's face fall under the umbrella of facial recognition software, a complicated industry. Not only is there strict regulation around facial recognition software, but the technology relies on neural networks... and large databases. It is illegal to collect a database of facial features or photographs, but there are companies that have been caught doing exactly this. Those companies have been shut down, but it's hard to say how many companies are still doing this.

The practical utilities of AR go way beyond QR code scanning and facial recognition. There could be a future where AR technology on our digital devices replaces measuring tapes by using image data to get an accurate measurement between real-world points. This technology can also enhance online shopping by superimposing clothes, accessories, and other merchandise on users—kind of like a virtual dressing room, but the room is whatever room you happen to be in. Even real estate development and interior design companies are looking into AR so that they can view a site, design an interactive artist's rendering, and deliver a more accurate quote for a project, all without leaving their desk.

There may be a future in which we all have VR headsets and sign on to work from our breakfast tables, but I don't think this is as realistic as the future AR technology is waving in. AR technology has the potential to innovate so many industries, and so much sooner. In many ways, AR is already here and it's just a matter of time until we see who jumps on the bandwagon.

Now let's look at two more trends of Wild technology innovation worth paying close attention to: quantum computing, and gene editing and DNA sequencing.

Quantum Computing

Quantum computing is a fun topic to talk about, provided that's all we do—talk about it. For the purposes of building a tech company, you don't need anything more than a basic awareness and understanding of what quantum computing is so you can avoid simple mistakes, such as promising quantum computing in your pitch deck to investors. If you make such a promise, they will run as far away from you as possible. So, please lower your expectations regarding any sort of integration of quantum computing in the near future.

One hundred years ago, the concept of cell phones was ridiculous. Telephones already existed, but they were all physically connected through thousands of miles of cable. The idea that billions of humans would soon possess a little metal brick in their pocket that could precisely transmit their voice (and video) to a flying space computer that would rebound their communication in real time to another person's metal brick anywhere in the world was inconceivable. (To most people, the flying space computer, i.e. satellites, sounded more realistic than this mobile phone witchcraft, even though wireless radio technology existed.)

And yet, in 1973, less than 20 years after the USSR successfully launched Sputnik into orbit, Motorola invented the first cell phone, the DynaTAC 8000X. For scientists, developers, and researchers already in the field, this was a major breakthrough. For investors, this was a thrilling opportunity, albeit a bit premature—the first 1G network was still six years away from its conception in Japan, and a full decade away from hitting the United States. And for the average citizen, the technology was still hard to wrap one's head around.

To many people, cell phones might have seemed like black magic at first, but by the turn of the 21st century the reality was that cell phones were a common personal gadget.

Why this digression on cell phones? Because it's important to understand where we are on the timeline regarding quantum computing's development. Yes, the technology has proven to be mechanically feasible (and not just theoretical), but we are still a long way from quantum computers becoming available to the public. Compared to cell phones, we are still in the "launching first satellites into space" phase. The only big players are governments and a couple giant tech companies. In the case of quantum computers, the biggest players right now are Google, IBM, Microsoft, the American government, and the Chinese government.

So, if you think you can just jump into the game and compete, fuhgeddaboudit. Don't touch quantum computing unless you have a super genius on your team...or, if *you* are a super genius. If that's the case, then what are you doing reading this book!? If you're reading this book, quantum computing is not for you. Not yet. Give it a decade, and then reconsider. For now, let's focus on what quantum computing is, and why it's still worth our attention, even though we're not putting our money or resources anywhere near it.

What Is Quantum Computing?
The Power to Change Everything

Quantum computing is, in oversimplified terms, a way for computers to solve complex problems using an alternative mechanic, thus cutting computing times to a nominal fraction of what they are with traditional computing mechanics. (Yes, this is the oversimplified version. In fact, everything in this section is going to be oversimplified because I am not a quantum computing super genius either.) To scratch the surface of understanding how this works, we'll start by breaking down the difference between traditional computing and quantum computing.

The way computers traditionally solve problems is by performing functions. Let's use brute force hacking as an example because this will become relevant later. If you want to brute force hack an eight-character password, you simply program a code to run through all the possible permutations of passwords until one finally works. You can tell the program to prioritize certain combinations, like passwords with only one special character or one-to-two capital letters. Ultimately, the determining factor of the program's success is the speed of the computer—how fast can it run through possible combinations until it finds the right one?

In 2019, the world's fastest supercomputer was IBM's Summit, capable of performing 200 quadrillion operations per second.[4] Today, the fastest supercomputer, Frontier, can perform 1.102 quintillion operations per second.[5] Except supercomputers are essentially just huge processing machines with billions of transistors, which means their efficiency is directly tied to the level of uncertainty in a problem. A supercomputer would still require billions upon billions of years to hack a 256-bit private blockchain key. It is like telling the computer to sift through all the atoms in the universe to find the one atom that opens a door. Don't expect supercomputers to open any doors in this lifetime.

Quantum computers, on the other hand, do not solve problems by performing calculations. Instead, they observe the state of quantum particles in a controlled environment to see how the particles form to fit a set of parameters. So, rather than form hundreds of quadrillions of trial-and-error operations, the quantum computer performs one task to solve for one uncertainty.

What does this mean?

Well, as of 2019, it means that a quantum computer (or, at least Google's quantum computer) can solve in four minutes a problem that would occupy IBM's Summit for about 10,000 years.[6]

---

4 https://www.cnet.com/news/ibms-world-class-summit-supercomputer-gooses-speed-with-ai-abilities/

5 https://en.wikipedia.org/wiki/Frontier_(supercomputer)#:~:text=Frontier%20achieved%20an%20Rmax%20of,Henri%20supercomputer%20in%20November%202022.

6 https://medium.com/predict/googles-quantum-computer-is-about-158-million-times-faster-than-the-world-s-fastest-supercomputer-36df56747f7f

If you don't have any knowledge of quantum mechanics—the behavioral properties of subatomic particles—this kind of technology can sound a bit like witchcraft. So, at risk of sounding a bit like a dark magician, let me try to get a bit more technical. Because again, this technology is real, and it's really cool!

Quantum computers function by observing the state of a quantum bit, or qubit. These subatomic particles are not like the protons and neutrons of atoms, which can simply be observed (by electron microscopes, not the naked eye) in their natural state. Qubits don't technically have a natural state. They hold two states at the same time until they are observed, and then they "pick" a state. So, for computing purposes, they can be both 0 and 1 at the same time.

Imagine you have a four-digit passcode, and each digit is either a 0 or 1. There are sixteen possible combinations of passcodes (1111, 1110, 1101, etc.). A classical computer would hack the code by trying each of the combinations one at a time because the digits can only be 0s or 1s. However, since a qubit can be 0 and 1 simultaneously, a quantum computer only needs four qubits to have immediate access to all sixteen possible combinations.

To put things in perspective, a quantum computer with 300 qubits could calculate for every atom in the known universe. And, as of November 2022, IBM's quantum computer Osprey is functional with 433 qubits. So, if you're locked out of your digital wallet and can't access your $500,000 in Bitcoin because you forgot your private key, give IBM a call.

Quantum computers are the greatest threat to cryptography, and therefore blockchain. While some private keys have way more than 256 bits, it's not unrealistic to think that quantum computers will be able to hack private keys of any complexity in the next 10-15 years. In anticipation of this problem, there are companies working right now to transition from regular encryption mechanics to quantum encryption mechanics.

In summary, the main function of a quantum computer is to find states that satisfy certain conditions. The mechanics are not sequential, like traditional computing, but to solve for uncertainty by fitting a specified state. Given enough qubits and enough creative programming, a whole universe of problems previously thought impossible becomes instantly solvable. This will change every industry, but the industry I'm most excited to see affected by quantum computing is the last one we will talk about in this book: gene editing and DNA sequencing.

Gene Editing & DNA Sequencing

Gene editing and DNA sequencing has been a field of innovation for decades. But with a combination of other Wild technologies reaching a stage of functional utility, the practical applications of this field are tallying up. And these aren't just fun practical applications for consumers to play around with on their smartphones, but applications that can save millions of lives.

The sequencing of the human genome is such a mysterious and fascinating field that's full of complications, but also incredible breakthroughs. For example, in February 2022, two people diagnosed with leukemia were determined to be in remission after a 10-year therapy in which they were treated with lab-modified immune cells.

The process was long and tedious, but what scientists ultimately did was edit one unit in the cancer cell's DNA. Just one! It's crazy when you think about it because it begs the question: How did the scientists figure out which unit to target?

As a tech guy, it's easy for me to think of DNA as nature's program for life. We still don't understand the full mechanics, but we know the parts and can deduce which parts dictate which functionality. And if we can fix the dysfunctional parts, then we can essentially fix biological problems the same way developers debug a piece of software. All we need is the ability to make edits, and the knowledge of where to make edits.

We cannot look at gene editing without also looking at DNA sequencing. They technically use two different technologies, but their utilities are so dependent on each other that they essentially combine to make up one field. Scientists started experimenting with gene editing technology in the mid- to late-1900s, but the Human Genome Project (HGP)—in which all the DNA of the human genome was mapped and sequenced—didn't reach its conclusion until 2003. The last twenty years have seen some incredible progress, but other technologies are speeding up the rate at which this field develops life-saving solutions.

The HGP gave scientists the data needed to identify which

DNA unit in the leukemia cells must be targeted for a potential cure. However, having a full database only speeds up the process so much. The database has tens of thousands of gene sequences, which are made up of billions of base DNA pairs. Computers can only sort through the data so quickly, and experiments to test hypotheses can only be performed so fast.

But what if we had technology that could study the database and understand it better than humans can? Quantum computing could solve for uncertainty rather than compute through the seemingly infinite solutions one-by-one. We could ask a computer, "What gene is mutated in this rare cancer?" And, based on the result, a machine would estimate which proteins must be constructed to edit the genes in the cancer cells. It's possible, with the help of quantum computing and AI, the next cure for cancer won't take a decade to develop.

Wild Tech: Helping or Hurting the Future?

The fact of the matter is that we don't know what the future will bring, but with this progress in Wild technology innovation, every possibility is on the table. From connecting others from all walks of life through metaverses, to envisioning better spaces in the real world with AR, to experimenting with life-like graphics in VR—there are still innovations to come.

Of course, there are multiple uses of innovation, some that help and others that hurt. Cambridge Analytica used AI innovation for nefarious purposes. Roblox entertains swaths of people in a virtual space, but is it adding or taking away from young people's ability to connect with others in a meaningful way? While I ask the *what ifs* about cures to cancer, others will ask the *what ifs* about mutating genes to extend the lives of evil dictators.

Despite the potential harms, I choose to be hopeful. There has always been evil in the world, but there has not always been so many wild possibilities to enact some good. The right tech has the power to save, not just one life, but millions—and Wild tech certainly has the power to improve the lives of billions.

Chapter 12:
Conclusion

We've explored Simple, Custom, and Wild products, as well as the major categories of Wild technology. Where do you go from here?

Upon your reading, you may get excited about one category or another. Dig deeper into whichever product, category, or field captures your interest the most. Let your excitement drive you. However, I want to reiterate three important things. Then, we'll bring this book to a close by looking toward the future (what's in store for tech companies) and looking at the present (what you can do to build a successful product today).

Three Key Takeaways

1. Avoid unnecessary risks during the MVP stage.

Given the choice between hiring a developer to write your code and buying a copy of code through CodeCanyon for $200, choose the latter. When you're going through the MVP stage, always defer to no-code platforms or cloning code first. Remember, you must prove the viability of your idea *before* you invest tens of thousands of dollars in developing it. Start with as little risk as possible because, as we've seen, early mistakes will haunt you and become big expensive mistakes later down the road.

2. Control the urge to over-delegate.

As you follow the growth of your product, the increasing tasks and responsibilities can start to feel overwhelming. At this point, too many non-technical entrepreneurs jump the gun and hire a developer or CTO to start taking over product-related matters. This is a mistake.

Remember, this is *your* product and *your* business. Unless you want to cough up 40-50 percent ownership early on— which is rarely ever necessary—be as involved as possible. Research your competitors for solutions. Experiment with API integrations. Take full ownership of your product in the early stages so you can continue to stay involved in the later stages.

3. Keep up-to-date with technology innovations in your industry.

At the end of the day, you must understand your product. This means understanding the technology on a deeper level. Your CTO can eventually manage the daily responsibilities, but you are responsible for learning about the core technology your product uses and for keeping pace with innovations in your industry. You don't need to know how to code, but you need to learn what you can about developments in your industry, your competitors, your company's workflow, related technologies that can be integrated, new ways your product can offer innovative utility to users, and so forth.

This book may serve as a guide, or cheat sheet, for getting started and moving your company through the phases of growth. However, keeping yourself up-to-date on the specifics of your product and its technology is an art. And *it is your responsibility*. Luckily, it can be fun! Remember, with technological progress, and the more that Wild technology matures (think LLMs and AI tools), the easier it will be for non-technical users to build complex Custom and Simple products: with no-code tools, AI helpers (agents), etc.

Looking Ahead: The Future of Tech Companies

In this book we covered three categories of tech products—Simple, Custom, and Wild. To recap, a Simple product is something anyone can build with the integration of other Custom or Wild products. Custom products require skilled engineers to develop, stabilize, and scale them. And Wild products require nothing less than technical genius and millions of dollars. This is the state of technology products and technology companies today, but how might this change in the future? After all, these categories are not necessarily fixed.

I think there is a near future in which there are no Custom

products. Yes, the bulk of this book is about starting a tech company around a Custom product, but Wild technology is only becoming more powerful and more accessible. It is easier than ever for non-technical entrepreneurs to build high-utility Simple products.

In the future, and with the help of AGI tools, companies may not need teams of developers to write code and address technical debt. So, instead of hiring software developers, human resources might function more as AI integration developers. Teams will likely get smaller, thus reducing the cost of more technical products.

And as for CTOs…their place in this future is a bit unclear. It seems to me that the market is moving toward consolidation. This means more technical responsibility will fall on the shoulders of the founders, and not the CTOs.

Future reorganization of tech companies might not be this extreme. I expect, at the very least, that roles will change. For this reason alone, I urge you to keep up with the developments of Wild technology and consider how those developments translate to your company, your product and your company's organization in the present.

Get the Best Out of Your Tech Company Today

I want to repeat an idea I've stated earlier in this book: focus on developing your product to provide practical utility to your customers. And, when the ride gets crazy and tough, enlist the support of your CTO, technical partners, or other technical professionals in your network.

When you think you're ready to build, integrate, or utilize some new technology, talk about it! Host brainstorm meetings. Get other people's perspectives. Heck, ask the geekiest teenager you know about the viability of your idea. You might just be surprised by how much valuable feedback they offer.

Technological innovation is rapid and constant, and it can be tempting to jump on new trends immediately. Don't be impulsive. But do have conversations and be systematic. No matter how complex the technology, or how sexy the product, human-to-human communication will always drive how well a tech company runs. In that spirit, here is one thing that you can be doing today to drive your company's success: **Have a monthly tech strategy meeting led by your CTO or tech partner.**

My best clients have strategy meetings *every week,* if not every day. They have an agenda and they regularly cycle through a long list of technical questions with their team so that technical strategy is always at the forefront of their minds.

Not all questions are relevant for various stages of the product development, but here is an exhaustive list of questions that you and your team should be asking during your meetings (feel free to skip non relevant ones):

- *How are you doing? How is the team?* Don't forget that the people on your team are people. Burnout is common at tech companies and even if you can't think of a way to avoid it in the short-term, simply acknowledging it can have a meaningful impact on your team's morale.

- ***How's scalability? How is technical debt?*** If you don't have a system for addressing your technical debt, then you are not ready to scale. Get a system in place to manage your technical debt as soon as you can. The rewards for making your business model scalable will be worth it.

- ***How is our process going to look when we scale?*** The more your infrastructure expands, the more hands you will need to manage it. And someone will usually need to be responsible for the increasing number of hands. Have a plan for how the organization of your company will evolve as you hire more people and make them responsible for various parts of your business.

- ***What are the most recent innovations in our field? What types of integrations can we benefit from?*** Don't silo your company, or your company will suffocate. When new technology becomes available and you believe your business can benefit from it, talk to your team about integrating it.

- ***What are competitors doing with technology? How do we feel about that?*** Make sure you have a pulse on your competitors' developments. Learn from what they are doing. You may not always have to react to what they are doing, but sometimes you do. And sometimes you just need to discuss whether your competitors are aware of your company's developments. If you're ahead, try to stay ahead for as long as possible.

- ***What can we do to stay competitive and keep our technology defensible? Is anything patentable?*** (Your CTO or tech partner has to constantly check this!) If your tech team develops something entirely innovative, jump on it immediately. Make sure it stays contained in your company long enough to patent it, and patent it as fast as possible.

- ***What kind of data can we collect? How can we use the data?*** This may involve conversations with a legal team, but your company's database can be a huge asset. Some companies are acquired simply because another company wants their database. Your data is part of your defensibility, so be proactive about how you use it and how you protect it.

- ***How secure is our platform? Are we protected from penetration or other attacks? What are our internal security measures to prevent social hacking?*** Address both internal and external risk factors. It's a balance between accessing enough company data to complete a task or do a job, but giving everyone access to all company files is highly risky. Not only could your employees exploit the data, one hacked employee means the whole company could crumble. Take measures to prevent outsiders (and insiders) from stealing your information. The more success you have, the more attractive you will look to people who are willing to break laws to get ahead. Be strategic.

- ***Are your R&D efforts protected by design?*** Are the

best people on your team incentivized to stay on your team? If not, are they under NDAs? Cross your T's and dot your I's here because there's no point in innovating new technology if the people who innovate it suddenly jump ship and take it elsewhere.

- *Do our technologies run the risk of falling behind?* If the market is moving away from your technology, be honest: Can you fight the market? Usually, the answer is no. Keep up with trends and see how you can ensure your product is always delivering real utility to your customers.

- *What is our budget for technology? What part of our budget is for scalability, improving infrastructure and architecture, and performance?* There's no point in doing the work to develop and stabilize your product if you cannot afford to bring it to scale. Plan ahead, use the tools available to you, and be as cost-effective as possible. Always ask your CTO or tech partners about current and anticipated costs.

- *How are we measuring and monitoring the perfor-mance of our engineers and other members of the tech team?* If your high-level engineers don't have managerial experience, you need to make sure they have precise systems in place to track KPIs and keep projects on schedule. Prioritize objectives and iterate on your workflows and processes. Don't let anyone hammer a nail more than is needed.

- *How does our brand or product look from a hiring per-*

spective? It doesn't matter how enthusiastic your team is if it can't grow. In order to hire and retain competitive talent, you need to be aware of how your company looks from the outside. Would you want to work at your company? If the answer is not a resounding yes, then you must consider what you can do to make it so.

- *Are we ready for a technology audit?* An audit can make or break your company's growth, so work closely with your CTO to stay on top of this. What security measures need to be in place? How is the data collected and managed? How do you use the data? Audits are not a big mystery, so do your research and be prepared to meet the requirements of any tests or investigations.

- *Are we paying market salaries?* This is pretty cut-and-dry, but it blows my mind how often business owners neglect to pay people fairly. If your business model cannot afford to pay people fairly, then your business model is broken. Fix it or watch as your best and brightest people take their skills elsewhere, to a company with a business model that can afford them.

Finally, there is one non technical question that I regularly ask my colleagues:

How can we make Aleph One the best place to work?

I don't just ask this question, but I also answer it. The workplace is where you and your employees spend the most time. Is the job fulfilling, or does it drain the life from you? If you as a founder do not love your job, then the same can probably be said for your employees. By asking this question, of yourself and your team, you will regularly surface actions you can take to make your workplace the best it can be.

When your team is fulfilled is when you can get the best out of your company.